F

The
Liberal Tradition

A Da Capo Press Reprint Series

FRANKLIN D. ROOSEVELT
AND THE ERA OF THE NEW DEAL

GENERAL EDITOR: FRANK FREIDEL
Harvard University

The *Liberal* *Tradition*

A FREE PEOPLE
AND A
FREE ECONOMY

By
LEWIS W. DOUGLAS

DA CAPO PRESS • NEW YORK • 1972

Library of Congress Cataloging in Publication Data

Douglas, Lewis Williams, 1894—
    The liberal tradition.
    (Franklin D. Roosevelt and the era of the New Deal)
    Originally delivered as the Godkin lectures at
Harvard University, May 6-10, 1935.
    1. U.S.—Economic conditions—1918-1945. 2. Industry
and state—U.S. 3. Finance—U.S. 4. Collectivism. 5. U.S.—
Economic policy—1933-1945.
    I. Title. II. Series. III. Series: Godkin lectures,
Harvard University, 1935.
HC106.3.D654 1972   330.973'0917   77-171382
ISBN 0-306-70376-9

This Da Capo Press edition of *The Liberal Tradition*
is an unabridged republication of the first edition
(second printing) published in New York in 1935.

Published by Da Capo Press, Inc.
A Subsidiary of Plenum Publishing Corporation
227 W. 17th St., New York, New York 10011

THE
Liberal Tradition

THE
Liberal Tradition

A FREE PEOPLE
AND A
FREE ECONOMY

By
LEWIS W. DOUGLAS

D. VAN NOSTRAND COMPANY, Inc.
250 FOURTH AVENUE,   NEW YORK
1935

THE CONTENTS

OF THIS BOOK WERE DELIVERED AS THE

GODKIN LECTURES

AT

HARVARD UNIVERSITY

MAY 6, 8, 9 AND 10, 1935

PREFACE

This small volume contains a series of four lectures delivered as the Godkin Lectures at Harvard University on the sixth, eighth, ninth and tenth of May, 1935.

I am sensible of their deficiencies as lectures and I am aware that many of these deficiencies are magnified by their publication in book form. In covering such a broad field in the limited space of four lectures it has been impossible to avoid making certain assumptions, to discuss subjects which should be discussed, and adequately to analyze others. Taxation, for example, is not mentioned. And in the last lecture, in dealing with the tariff and the regimented order which must result from a policy of isolation, the discussion is inadequate.

It is, therefore, not amiss here to point out that in an isolated economy, i.e., an economy in which the domestic surpluses can not be sold abroad, the exporting industries must be compelled by government order to restrict production. As cases in point, the growing of cotton, the production of certain kinds of textiles, the manufacture of automobiles, in time would all be subjected to complete government regulations designed to restrict production to domestic demand. The regulation of them by the government eventually would have such effects on collateral industries that they, too, would be subject to the same type of control. This, in turn, would

eventually exert pressure on our entire economic
life and lead to complete regulation if not to government ownership. Thus a policy of excessive tariff
protection leads to a Collective State. This, it seems
to me, is in part a rationalization of some of the
forces we are now experiencing, some of the acts
which are now being undertaken, and some of the
fallacies so prevalently accepted.

It may very well be that in the second lecture the
criticisms of a Collective State are too severe, at
least in what may be its initial stages. And yet it
seems to me that in its final development it must
be approximately as pictured.

In the discussion of the present fiscal policy no
mention has been made of the Agricultural Adjustment Administration payments. The omission is attributable to what appears to be the fact that, while
in the past, payments have not been balanced by
receipts from the processing taxes, in the future,
there will be an equilibrium between disbursements
and revenues.

In the last lecture it is conceivable that an unat-
tainable objective has been set up. It may well be
that the forces are too strong, too irresistible, to
permit of a change of direction toward what seems
to me to be real liberalism. Yet however strong,
however irresistible these forces may be, the struggle
against them is worth undertaking.

In some measure these lectures are a criticism of
my own acts while in Congress. For, though opposed to high tariffs, I once participated in obtaining protection for copper, principally because almost

everything else was protected, and partially because
the entire State which I represented had been
worked up to a fever pitch in advocacy of it. And
on another occasion I voted for the original Reconstruction Finance Corporation Act. My misgivings
and doubts were grave. Yet it appeared to me at
the time that it was appropriate to vote for a measure which represented a cooperative effort between
the two Parties.

Momentous events of historic significance have
occurred since the lectures were delivered.

The Supreme Court of the United States, in
unanimous decisions of profound importance, has
declared to be unconstitutional two acts of the present administration. One voided part of the National
Industrial Recovery Act, while the other, of almost
equal significance, declared to be invalid the removal of a member of the Federal Trade Commission, created by Congress as a quasi-judicial body
to perform certain specified duties.

In the latter case, known as the Humphrey case,
notwithstanding statutory provisions expressly defining the grounds on which removal could be
effected, resignation was requested for the reason
given in a communication of the Chief Executive to
Commissioner Humphrey, dated August 31, 1933:

"You will, I know, realize that your mind and my
mind do not go along together on either the policies
or the administering of the Federal Trade Commission, and, frankly, I think it is best for the people
of this country that I should have a full confidence."

In a unanimous opinion the Court held that the

Executive had no such power of removal, and, among
other things, stated: [1]

"If Congress is without authority to prescribe
causes for removal of members of the Trade Commission and limit executive power of removal ac-
cordingly, that power at once becomes practically
all inclusive in respect of civil officers, with the
exception of the judiciary provided for by the
Constitution. The Solicitor General at the bar, apparently recognizing this to be true, with com-
mendable candor agreed that his view in respect of
the removability of members of the Federal Trade
Commission necessitated a like view in respect of
the Interstate Commerce Commission and the Court
of Claims. *We are thus confronted with the serious
question whether not only the members of these
quasi-legislative and quasi-judicial bodies, but the
judges of the legislative court of claims, exercising
judicial power . . . continue in office only at the
pleasure of the President.*

"We think it plain under the Constitution that
illimitable power of removal is not possessed by the
President in respect of officers of the character of
those just named. The authority of Congress, in
creating quasi-legislative or quasi-judicial agencies,
to require them to act in discharge of their duties
independently of executive control, cannot well be
doubted; and that authority includes, as an appropriate incident, power to fix the period during which
they shall continue, and to forbid their removal except for cause in the meantime. *For it is quite evident that one who holds his office only during the
pleasure of another cannot be depended upon to
maintain an attitude of independence against the
latter's will.*"

[1] Italics mine.

The language of the Court makes only too evident the profound implications in the Humphrey case.

In addition to these two decisions, both the Court and the Constitution itself are now being subjected to attack. It is being argued that the Court should have no power to declare an act of Congress to be unconstitutional. What this argument really means is that the Constitution should be made meaningless. For if the Court be denied its right to declare an act of Congress to be repugnant to the basic law of the land, then the Congress is automatically empowered — among other things — to destroy the States, to deny the right of trial, and even to abolish the courts themselves. Certainly it would destroy the protection individuals or even States now have against oppressive acts of the government and would clear the way toward the establishment of a completely tyrannical State.

Throughout history man has struggled to escape from the oppression of arbitrary acts of majorities, of minorities and of governments themselves. Our Supreme Court and our Constitution — however much at times various groups may have thought them to be wrong—are the peculiar creatures of the American genius to provide protection against the very despotism from which the Pilgrims and all subsequent immigrants fled.

On this subject spoke Woodrow Wilson, a great liberal:[1]

"Our courts are the balance-wheel of our whole

[1] Woodrow Wilson, "Constitutional Government in the United States," pp. 142-3 (Columbia University Press, N. Y., 1911).

constitutional system; and ours is the only constitutional system so balanced and controlled. Other constitutional systems lack complete poise and certainty of operation because they lack the support and interpretation of authoritative, undisputable courts of law. It is clear beyond all need of exposition that for the definite maintenance of constitutional understandings it is indispensable, alike for the preservation of the liberty of the individual and for the preservation of the integrity of the powers of the government, that there should be some non-political forum in which those understandings can be impartially debated and determined. That forum our courts supply. There the individual may assert his rights; there the government must accept definition of its authority. There the individual may challenge the legality of governmental action and have it judged by the test of fundamental principles, and that test the government must abide; there the government can check the too aggressive self-assertion of the individual and establish its power upon lines which all can comprehend and heed. The constitutional powers of the courts constitute the ultimate safeguard alike of individual privilege and of governmental prerogative. It is in this sense that our judiciary is the balance-wheel of our entire system; it is meant to maintain that nice adjustment between individual rights and governmental powers which constitutes political liberty.

"I am not now thinking of the courts as the lawyer thinks of them, as places of technical definition and business adjustment, where the rights of individuals as against one another are debated and determined; but as the citizen thinks of them, as his safeguard against a too arrogant and teasing use of power by the government, an instrument of politics, —of liberty."

Another significant event has occurred since these lectures were delivered. There was held in Washington on May thirty-first, a press conference in which the Court's *unanimous* decision invalidating the National Recovery Industrial Act was severely criticized. According to press accounts the interstate commerce clause of the Constitution was discussed in the light of the Court's action and the Court was discussed in the light of the interstate commerce clause. The inference was given, if it was not expressly stated in fact, that the decision carried us back to the "horse and buggy days," and that the Constitution should be changed so as to permit of the centralization in Washington of complete power over the economic system of the country.

On the subject of the interstate commerce clause, too, and its significance to our form of government, Woodrow Wilson expressed himself:[1]

"The Constitution was not meant to hold the Government back to the time of horses and wagons, the time when postboys carried every communication that passed from merchant to merchant, when trade had few long routes within the nation and did not venture in bulk beyond neighborhood transactions. The United States have clearly from generation to generation been taking on more and more the characteristics of a community; more and more have their economic interests come to seem common interests; and the courts have rightly endeavored to make the Constitution a suitable instrument of the national life, extending to the things that are now

[1] Woodrow Wilson, "Constitutional Government in the United States," pp. 169-171, 191-192 (Columbia University Press, N. Y., 1911).

common the rules that it established for similar things that were common at the beginning.

"The real difficulty has been to draw the line where this process of expansion and adaptation ceases to be legitimate and becomes a mere act of will on the part of the Government, served by the courts. The temptation to overstep the proper boundaries has been particularly great in interpreting the meaning of the words 'commerce among the several states.' Manifestly, in a commercial nation almost every item of life directly or indirectly affects commerce, and our commerce is almost all of it upon the grand scale. There is a vast deal of buying and selling, of course, within the boundaries of each state, but even the buying and selling which is done within a single state constitutes in our day but a part of that great movement of merchandise along lines of railway and watercourse which runs without limit and without regard to political jurisdiction. State commerce seems almost impossible to distinguish from interstate commerce. It has all come to seem part of what Congress may unquestionably regulate, though the makers of the Constitution may never have dreamed of anything like it and the tremendous interests which it affects. Which part of the complex thing may Congress regulate?

"Clearly, any part of the actual movement of merchandise and persons from state to state. May it also regulate the conditions under which the merchandise is produced which is presently to become the subject matter of interstate commerce? May it regulate the conditions of labor in field and factory? Clearly not, I should say; and I should think that any thoughtful lawyer who felt himself at liberty to be frank would agree with me. For that would be to destroy all lines of division between the field of state legislation and the field of federal legislation. Back of the conditions of labor in the field and in the fac-

tory lie all the intimate matters of morals and of
domestic and business relationship which have
always been recognized as the undisputed field of
state law, and these conditions that lie back of labor
may easily be shown to have their part in determining the character and efficiency of commerce between
the states. If the federal power does not end with
the regulation of the actual movement of trade, it
ends nowhere, and the line between state and federal
jurisdiction is obliterated. But this is not universally seen or admitted. It is, therefore, one of
the things upon which the conscience of the nation
must take test of itself, to see if it still retains that
spirit of constitutional understanding which is the
only ultimate prop and support of constitutional
government. It is questions of this sort that show
the true relation of our courts to our national character and our system of government. . . .

"It would be fatal to our political vitality really
to strip the states of their powers and transfer them
to the federal government. It cannot be too often
repeated that it has been the privilege of separate
development secured to the several regions of the
country by the Constitution, and not the privilege of
separate development only, but, also, that other more
fundamental privilege that lies back of it, the
privilege of independent local opinion and individual
conviction, which has given speed, facility, vigor and
certainty to the processes of our economic and
political growth. To buy temporary ease and con-
venience for the performance of a few great tasks
of the hour at the expense of that would be to pay
too great a price and to cheat all generations for
the sake of one."

No one can charge Woodrow Wilson with being a
Tory or a reactionary, yet he definitely takes a posi-

tion identical with that of the Supreme Court and points out the consequences of centralizing power.

While the comments contained in these lectures on the National Recovery Administration are now temporarily immaterial, the events of the last few weeks should remove all doubt that the Administration's design—conscious or unconscious—is that of a Collective system.

The Agricultural Adjustment Administration and its clarifying amendments vest in the Executive or his administrative officer complete power over agriculture and the processing industries.

The National Industrial Recovery Act, now temporarily deceased, vested in the Executive complete powers over all industry and commerce.

The Securities Act tends to make of the Federal government the exclusive capitalist.

The Wagner Labor Bill vests in the Federal government the power to regulate all employer-employee relations, and even to dictate the terms of settlements.

The Guffey Coal Bill vests in the Federal government complete authority over the coal mining industry and practically nationalizes it.

The Banking Bill vests in the Executive complete control over credit, and socializes bank deposits.

Confiscation of gold, the control over the central banking system, the socialization of bank deposits, and the policy of deliberate spending, coincide with the acts of the Soviet undertaken after the fall of the Kerensky regime.

If, however, in spite of the perfect pattern made

by these and other measures, there remain any
doubts of the design, the press conference of May
thirty-first dispels them, for it evidenced two things—
a deep dissatisfaction with the one body, i.e., the
Supreme Court, which alone assures Constitutional
government and protection against oppression; and
a desire to vest in Washington complete control over
the intimate acts of political subdivisions and
thereby to destroy the very foundation of the American
system.

In the light of these events, the issue as defined
in these lectures is now amply clarified.

LEWIS W. DOUGLAS

JUNE 21, 1935.

CONTENTS

INTRODUCTION

I have selected as the title of these lectures, "The Liberal Tradition." And I have used the word "liberal" because it is as applicable in its general meaning of freedom as it is in its meaning of opposition to an existing order.

Permit me to explain at the very beginning of these discussions that I make no claim to the possession of oracular wisdom, that I cannot with any degree of honesty occupy or stand upon the pedestal of an expert, that I have no intention to be either pontifical or dogmatic, and that I am incapable of offering anything of intellectual profundity.

I merely propose to express simply and directly a point of view which seems to be gradually disappearing from human consciousness. That it may be popular with no group I am fully aware. But neither hope of approval nor fear of disapproval should deter its presentation.

It is born of doubts and suspicions, experience of the present and, within the limitations of my mental powers, analysis of the past. It matters not at what angle it may cross present moods nor run counter to popular movements—convictions can yield to neither.

It is not strange that men's minds should be bewildered by the turmoil of the period in which they now live, for the confusion is great, and few there

are who seize from a hectic life of speed the occasion
to contemplate calmly the world about them. Caught
by the "babble of the babbling box and a babbling
world," man is again demonstrating, as he has demonstrated many times before, his peculiar ability to
lose his sense of proportion, and to forget that the
only characteristic which distinguishes him from
other forms of animal life is an alleged power to
think.

Perhaps, through all the noise and empty phrases,
the passions and the hatreds, the prejudices and the
emotions, some gleam of light, some clarification of
thought, some crystallization of conviction, some re-
generation of character, some faith, will penetrate to
dispel the fogs of doubt and of confusion.

The stakes are high, higher perhaps than they
have ever been before. Western civilization conceivably hangs in the balance. What we now do
here may have profound consequences. Already three
major powers of the Western world have deserted
from the family of parliamentary governments and
free peoples. All are in the throes of an economic
distress which, if it does not soon begin to disappear,
must make for serious social and political disturb-
ances. And over the entire world hang the dark
clouds of war. Everywhere men's hopes are on
America. To her men's eyes are turned. In part, it
is upon her acts that the recovery of the world rests.

And so it seems to me that we Americans should
begin to think and to think carefully on the general
subject of the kind of a social and economic system
under which we want to live, that we should decide

whether we are willing consciously to discard the basic principles of freedom on which this country was built, and in which we have heretofore expressed our faith, or whether we will attempt with equal consciousness and integrity to stand fast; whether the case against those principles is stronger than is the case for them, whether mankind will be happier by throwing these principles overboard or by insisting on the performance of those acts which again must make them vital living things.

This is the basic question. We cannot long ignore it. For if we delay too long we may discover that the forces engendered by acts already taken have so broken the reins of control that they have started, with the bit between their teeth, on a wild run toward an unknown destination.

These discussions will attempt a consideration of this issue and will be divided into four lectures, the first entitled "The Sins of the Past," the second "A Planned Economy and The Oppressive State," the third, "Dictatorship and a Fiscal Policy," and the fourth, "A Free People and a Free Economy."

THE LIBERAL TRADITION

I

It may be of some help in the process of making
the determination to examine somewhat hastily and
in rather broad outline the sins of the past, for mistakes committed may throw some light on mistakes
to be avoided.

It is not uncommon to hear and to read the statement: "Capitalism has failed; capitalism must go."
In a certain sense the system has failed, but was
that system a free capitalistic one, or was it but a
modern imitation of a Seventeenth Century pattern?

It seems to me that an analysis of the economy
which existed in this country from the close of the
second decade of this century until the end of the
third discloses four dominant characteristics and
fallacies.

The first of these was exorbitantly high tariffs. It
is probably true that a country which has developed
its economy behind high import duties cannot sustain the economic shock of a complete and sudden
removal of these indirect subsidies. But however
that may be, the defects and painful consequences of
a high protectionist policy, particularly when applied to a nation which had become a creditor, should
not pass without both notice and emphasis.

1

The movement for high tariffs—in some instances embargo tariffs—was given its momentum in large measure by marginal producers who could not survive the test of competitive forces. They sought and obtained an indirect subsidy from the government—collected from the consumer—to make secure and profitable the capital invested in the marginal enterprises.

One of the effects was to maintain for a while to the benefit of the inefficient enterprise, an artificial price level for, and income from, manufactured articles. Coincident with the artificial support of an industrial price level by high protectionist tariffs, the price of agricultural commodities, a large part of which were sold in the world market, was slowly falling. Thus the protectionist policy tended to create a discrepancy between the two great factions in our national economy—agriculture and industry—and tended to impose upon the farmer a higher price for the thing which he bought and a lower price for the thing which he sold.

But this is not all which the high tariff policy succeeded in accomplishing.

The United States emerged from the War period as the great creditor nation of the world. It was a new rôle and one which, because of lack of experience, we neither recognized nor, if we recognized it, fully comprehended. We did not appreciate as a nation that, to the extent to which we prevented our exports from being paid with goods, to the same extent we must drain gold from the rest of the world. Nor did we appreciate that, to the extent to which we drained gold from the rest of the world, to the same extent we would hasten a collapse of world currencies. Nor did we appreciate that, to the extent to which we, by our policy encouraged a collapse of world currencies, to the same extent we would set in motion deflationary forces within the United States and throughout the world. Nor did we understand—apparently we do not understand it now—that these very deflationary forces would induce governments to impose tariffs, quotas, embargoes, allotments, exchange restrictions—and the whole gamut of similar devices—in futile attempts to halt the deflation and thereby to protect their national economies and currencies. Nor do we understand that the very devices used diminished the demand for and volume of goods to be exchanged, consequently intensifying the deflationary disease that they sought to cure.

A second major dominant characteristic of our economic system of the '20's was the governmental sanction to illegal price fixing. Or, to state it in different terms and perhaps more truthfully, an indifference on the part of the Federal government to the provisions of the Sherman Anti-Trust Laws. This winking, as it were, at the provisions of the Law designed to enforce competition permitted certain industries in the United States to maintain a price level for certain commodities which could not have obtained had competitive forces been permitted to work their will. Thus, as a result of this policy, the discrepancy between agriculture and industry was intensified. For the fixing of prices was merely another act which had the effect of imposing upon the farmer the burden of paying a higher price for the things he purchased while the price of things which he sold was tending to fall.

The third major characteristic of the period under consideration was an ill-advised managed currency. In 1925, Great Britain returned to the gold standard at its old gold parity under the illusion that it was a parity which could be maintained without major internal adjustments of costs. At the same time the United States, because of its tariff policy and because of its new status as a creditor nation, was drawing gold in the settlement of its favorable balance of payments.[1]

Coincidentally, a complicated situation developed abroad. France had passed through her post-war period of inflation into one of de facto stabilization, and capital which had previously fled from Paris was returning from London. The money rates in France consequently fell. The Bank of England instead of halting the outflow by raising the rate —in other words, instead of playing the gold standard according to the rules of the game—followed suit and lowered its rate. Sterling was approximately $4.85, or below par, and England was rapidly losing gold both to the East and to the West. In an effort to reverse the Western flow, to assist sterling, and to

[1] Harold L. Reed, "Federal Reserve Policy, 1921-1930" (McGraw-Hill Book Co., New York), p. 96.
Increase in monetary gold stocks, 1927.

January	70 millions
February	20 millions
March	10 millions
April	10 millions

GOLD FLOW TO AND FROM THE UNITED STATES

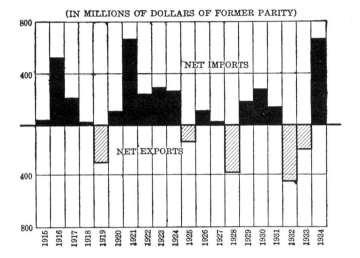

Net gold imports in 1934 reached a new high record of $1,132,-
000,000 (new parity). For purposes of comparison with imports of
previous years, this sum has been converted into dollars of the former
parity, and is thus shown on the accompanying chart. This chart
depicts the progressive accumulation of gold in the United States
during the past twenty years.

The first heavy movement of gold to the United States during this
period occurred in 1915-17, when the Allies were buying large quantities of foodstuffs and war materials in this country. The second
large importation occurred in 1920-24 and reflected the use of gold
by foreign debtors to discharge their American obligations. The
record-breaking imports of 1934 indicate in part a repatriation of
American funds which had been recently sent abroad to escape the
effects of currency depreciation.

The inflow of gold was checked temporarily in 1925, following ship-
ments of the metal to Germany after the negotiation of the Dawes
Plan Loan and the increased confidence in European currencies incident to Great Britain's return to the gold standard. In 1928 the
United States again lost a substantial amount of gold to Europe. It
was then the Federal Reserve Board's policy to encourage gold exports through a low bank rate, with a view to aiding the general
restoration of the international gold standard. The outflow of gold
in 1932-33 was due to a flight from the dollar during the financial
crisis of those years. (From Council on Foreign Relations, Inc.)

nullify our tariff policy with its gold sucking effects, we lowered our discount rate.[1] By September, 1927, all twelve Federal Reserve Banks had effected the reduction. Moreover, between July and December of 1927, the holdings of governments by the Reserve Banks were increased $218,000,000 through open market operations.[2]

It is interesting to note that the Chicago Federal Reserve Bank at first refused to lower the rate and that the Federal Reserve Board vetoed its action. Moreover, because industrial production had begun to decline slightly—not encouraging to those whose eyes were on the national election of 1928—and because the Secretary of the Treasury was quoted on March 27, 1927, as saying:[3]

"I see nothing to indicate that business will not continue to be good throughout the country. . . . There is an abundant supply of easy money which should take care of any contingencies that might arise. I do not look for any change in the Federal Reserve rediscount rate for some time to come because I can see no reason for changing it."
and:

"Brokers' loans give a very good insight into the stock market situation, and they appear in a very healthy state."

---

[1] To lower a discount rate makes money cheaper.

[2] Harold L. Reed, ''Federal Reserve Policy, 1921-1930'' (McGraw-Hill Book Co., New York), pp. 102-3, 122.

Open market operations in government obligations constitute purchases in the market by the Reserve System of government bonds and increase the amount of credit available, thus cheapening money.

[3] Harold L. Reed, ''Federal Reserve Policy, 1921-1930'' (McGraw-Hill Book Co., New York), pp. 105, 137.

—Because of these events it is not unreasonable to suspect that the Federal Reserve Board was not wholly free from political influences in encouraging the cheap money policy. Fairness requires, however, that there should here be recalled the consistent rumor that the Secretary of the Treasury later constantly voted to permit the Federal Reserve Banks to raise the discount rates and so to bring to an end the cheap money policy.

Also, it is not irrelevant to point out that the McFadden Banking Act which extended the use of national bank credit for capital and speculative purposes became a law on February 25, 1927. This aided the cheap money policy by providing an enlarged base of credit and new opportunities for the use of credit in ways which should have been satisfied by savings.

It must be said that the Federal Reserve Banks were fully aware of the hazards which they were taking, that they understood the dangers, but that they thought that they could control the situation which cheap money here might create in time to prevent a collapse.

They were apprehensive about the use in the speculative markets of credit generated by cheap money but they felt that they could raise the rates, sell governments and bills and thus contract credit before the "boom" had gone so far as to make a destructive deflation inevitable. When, however, they undertook to apply the brakes, memory of the popular antagonism to the deflationary acts of the System in 1920, and what now appears to have been strong resistance from political sources intervened to prevent taking effective measures of control in time to prevent the extremes to which the inflation went. Thus the situation got out of hand. The lowering of the rediscount rate and the open market operations of the Federal Reserve Banks therefore inaugurated a new period of cheap money in the United States.

There were two major effects of this policy:

It had the effect of bolstering artificially that part of our price structure already twice bolstered by high tariffs and price fixing, but which, despite these two, had begun a slow decline. Thus, the action of the Federal Reserve System was a third factor which tended to intensify the slowly widening discrepancy between the price of agricultural commodities and the price of manufactured ones.

The second effect was to create an excessive amount of credit, a part of which slopped over into speculative markets and a part of which encouraged the incurment of excessive debt for capital purposes and the production of goods at a cost which the price level, when its artificial supports were to collapse, could not maintain. Another way of stating the second result of the cheap money policy is to say that it initiated a period of wild inflation with almost all of the characteristics of such inflation except that of a rising commodity price level [1]—excessive credit, a rising stock market, and an industrial expansion which was neither financed in large part out of sav-

---

[1] The effect was probably to stabilize certain prices for a limited period when, if there had been no credit expansion, they would have fallen.

ings nor justified by the real as distinct from the artificial factors in the situation. To the public these all were crystallized in a wild orgy of security speculation.

And here it should be noted that the spirit of speculation was not limited to the canyons of the south end of Manhattan Island. It pervaded almost every city, village and hamlet in the country. It was encountered at almost every cross-road store and gasoline station.

It should be noted here, too, that in the early part of 1929, when the situation was still partially savable to the extent that if the proper thing had then been done the fall would not have been so great, the New York Federal Reserve Bank and several of the other Federal Reserve Banks discussed with and asked of the Federal Reserve Board in Washington permission to raise the discount rate.[1] I think it has been established and generally conceded to be true that the Federal Reserve Board in Washington acting under political influence refused to grant the request on the grounds that if granted deflation would have been induced. It was not until August of 1929, when the momentum had carried the boom to extraordinary speculative heights that the Federal Reserve Board acquiesced. It was then too late.

Here it seems to me not unimportant to bring together these first three major characteristics, i.e.,

[1] "Monetary Mischief," by George Buchan Robinson, published after these lectures were delivered but before they went to the press contains a full account of the controversy between the New York Federal Reserve Bank, the Federal Advisory Council and the Federal Reserve Board. It confirms everything here presented.

high tariffs, price fixing and cheap money, and to outline briefly a social and economic consequence of the three acting upon one another and upon the public mind.

High tariffs, in addition to their effects on currencies and agriculture, destroyed competition from without the United States, thus making more possible the second major characteristic—monopolistic practice of price fixing. The cheap money and tariff policies, coupled with price fixing, tended temporarily to stabilize a portion of our price level, to concentrate public attention on securities rather than on production and to whet a public appetite for pieces of paper. In this atmosphere smaller producers, witnessing what was apparently a stable price level, feeling the pressure of money to be made out of pieces of paper rather than out of production, lent themselves to exchanging ownership of their companies for ownership of securities in other companies. Thus mergers and the emission of the securities of merged corporations flourished and thus the three dominant characteristics together tended to concentrate means of production in the hands of a few and to encourage over-capitalization.

It was a system, too, into which many rigidities had crept. This is the fourth dominant major characteristic of the post-war decade.[1] The cheap money

[1] When capital is obtained through a bond, or a mortgage, the cost of the capital is fixed by the rate of interest. When, however, capital is obtained through common stocks or equities no fixed charge is incurred.

Political subdivisions cannot, of course, use the common stock method of obtaining capital.

policy encouraged the incurment of excessive debt by individuals as well as by corporations, thus making the cost of capital a rigid, unalterable cost of production. The disease spread like a pestilence. States and local political subdivisions became infected and, because of the excessive borrowing on bonds by them, taxes were raised to meet interest on the debt. This increased the cost of production for the industrialist, the miner, the merchant, and the farmer.[1]

It was a period in which the cost of labor had tended to become rigid. It was a period marked by barriers to the flow of goods. In other words, it was a period in which, through man's folly, and government activities, in part because of selfish interests, in part because of ignorance, the flexibility essential to a successful working of the profit system was so diminished that when the inevitable collapse came the necessary readjustments requisite to recovery had been at least in part inhibited.

This was the system, if it can be called a system, which failed. It was not a system of free competition; it was not a system of rugged individualism. On the contrary, in some measure at least, it was a system of degenerate capitalism in which capitalists of all grades and all classes sought the assistance of government, profited or attempted to profit by subsidies, endeavored to escape from the rigors of competition, so that the inefficient might survive—in short a system in which the capitalists advocated the

1 Evans Clark, ''The Internal Debts of the United States'' (The Macmillan Co., N. Y., 1933), pp. 10, 16.

things which must destroy the system in which they professed to believe. It was a period of wild inflation made wild by political influence. It was a period marked by man's ignorance of the operation of a great economy, a period marked by greed just as are all inflationary periods, a period in which the emphasis had become transferred in part from the acquisition of wealth by production to the acquisition of wealth by manipulation of pieces of paper. And it is not unnatural that this period should have been thus marked, for almost all post-war periods evidence the same characteristics of human folly. If my recollection be correct, the thirty-year period after the Napoleonic Wars in Europe was one in which the same type of phenomena, the same sort of folly, stalked the stage of human affairs. In our own history, the post Civil War period was not dissimilar. Inflation, speculation, watered capitalization, scandals in high places, "black Fridays" and "red Mondays," several members of the House of Representatives indicted of complicity in the Credit-Mobilier scandal, several members of the Senate suspected![1] It seems that wars, either because it is the war or the inflation induced by expenditures, do certain things to human character, obscure a sense of reality and dim a vision of ethics. But whatever the cause may be, the Post-War period in the United States is more or less characteristic of the previous inflationary periods in our history. It was a system,

---

[1] Lloyd Paul Styrker—"Andrew Johnson—A Study in Courage" (The Macmillan Company, New York, 1929), Ch. XVII "Credit Mobilier," p. 521.

a hybrid sort of an affair, predicated upon the general romanticism of cheap money, and governmentally supported subsidies and rigidities which collapsed—a system not dissimilar in many respects from its Seventeenth Century progenitor. And then, after the collapse, men found it difficult to face reality. They failed to appreciate that the thing which they were experiencing was of major importance. They clung to the romantic conception that prosperity was around the corner, defining prosperity as the hectic speculative period of 1929, and refused to face the bitter fact that penalties had to be paid for the economic excesses in which they had indulged. The Federal government itself requested of the utilities and great industrialists that they embark upon a spending program, and to a certain extent they complied with the request. It urged that wages be not reduced, and for a considerable period they were not. It erected a great mechanism to support financial institutions and railroads made weak by their acts, and by their own acts in many cases made unfit to survive. It attempted to maintain prices of agricultural commodities by artificial expedients. At the very time when a change of direction in our tariff policy should have been made, it went further in old directions, thus intensifying the deflationary forces. By almost every conceivable device man contrived to prevent adjustment of cost to prices, and so unwittingly prevented the recurrence of prospective profit and of employment.

But all the time, whatever the devices employed, the price of commodities continued to fall. Unemployment continued to increase; national income continued to decline. The Federal budget became more and more unbalanced and the inevitable end became more and more inevitable. The only effect of these anti-deflationary devices was to prevent the outward expression of deflation without curing the inner cause. The deflationary forces thus stored up behind the anti-deflationary structures finally swept over the dam in one great torrent.

II

A Planned Economy and the Oppressive State

There now are many who confuse the hectic Post-War period and the initial stages of the depression, which have been described, with the competitive system. In some cases the confusion can be attributed to ignorance. In some cases it can be attributed to deliberate design. But it is unimportant to what the confusion may be attributed. The fact is that many confuse the system which failed with the competitive system for profit, and they would substitute a social and economic system completely new to America for the one under which we have grown great. Some call it the substitution of a system of "serviceability" for a system of "vendability"— nice sounding words and phrases, plausible—a system to be operated by a "general staff," whatever a "general staff" may be, but presumably meaning a government bureau, although another term may be used to define it. Some call it a "Planned Economy," some a "New Economic Order." But however beautiful may be the words and phrases used and however the "general staff" may be defined— however seductively—the essence of the system to be substituted is one of complete regulation by the government eventually developing into State ownership, or one of immediate State ownership, whether through State corporations or through some other State agency is quite immaterial.

Many arguments are advanced by these various advocates. They have appeared before in one form or another in almost all previous industrial depressions. The first is that the world is overbuilt, that we have a productive capacity in excess of our capacity to consume under a capitalistic system, that there is therefore no need for capital investment. Consequently it is alleged that there will be no capital investment and that men will not find reemployment through the ordinary processes of a capitalistic profit system. I have said that this argument is not new. It appeared for example in 1819, in 1840, in the '80's of the last century, and in 1921. Sismondi stated the case in 1819:

"By an inherent contradiction in modern economic conditions, while their great wealth push the wealthy to build vast factories, their riches also exclude the products of these very great factories from the consumption of the rich. Those who receive the selling price of the merchandise, those who benefit from fabrication, are not the same as those who consume them. The production thus goes on accumulating while consumption is restrained. Overproduction is a fatal effect of contemporaneous economic organization." [1]

Horace Greeley referred to it in 1850:

"I trust no one here gives any heed to the mumbling of self-styled political economists about over-

[1] M. de Sismondi, "Les nouveaux principes d'economie politique ou de la richess dans ses rapports, avec la population" (2 vols. 8 vo., 1st ed., 1819).

production and kindred phrases with which counsel is darkened. Overproduction of what? Where? Can there be overproduction of food when so many, even in our midst, are suffering the pangs of famine? Overproduction of clothing and fabrics, while our streets swarm with men, women and children who are not half clad and who shiver through the night beneath the clothing they have worn by day? Overproduction of dwellings, when not half the families of our city have adequate and comfortable habitations, not to speak of that large class whose lodgings are utterly incompatible with decency and morality?"[1]

Carroll D. Wright, Commissioner of Labor in the Cleveland Administration, stated it in 1886:

"What is strictly necessary has been done often times to superfluity. This full supply of economic tools to meet the wants of nearly all branches of commerce and industry is the most important factor in the present industrial depression.

"It is true that the discovery of new processes of manufacture will undoubtedly continue, and this will act as an ameliorating influence, but it will not leave room for a marked extension, such as has been witnessed during the last fifty years, or afford a remunerative employment of the vast amount of capital which has been created during that period."[2]

David A Wells, in the middle eighties of the last century, ascribed the depression to the extraordinarily rapid increase in and improvement of the instrumentalities of production and distribution, "and to the fact that the supply of the great articles and

[1] N. Y. *Herald Tribune*, Jan. 27, 1935, Letter from Sam H. Seymour, Chattanooga, Tenn., Jan. 17, 1935.
[2] Report, U. S. Dept. of Labor, 1886.

instrumentalities of the world's use and commerce has increased, during the last ten or fifteen years, in a far greater ratio than the contemporaneous increase in the world's population, or of its immediate consuming capacity." [1]

David Friday in part stated the case in 1921:

"The demand for capital to be used in the promotion of new business enterprises will be comparatively slight during the next two years. . . . If we can produce 25 per cent more than the home consumer will purchase, and if industrial profits are lacking in consequence, there can be no great need for immediate expansion." [2]

The latest expression of this view is that of Rexford G. Tugwell:

"Our economic course has carried us from the era of economic development to an era which confronts us with the necessity for economic maintenance. In this period of maintenance, there is no scarcity of production. There is, in fact, a present capacity for more production than is consumable, at least under a system which shortens purchasing power while it is lengthening capacity to produce." [3]

[1] David A. Wells, "Recent Economic Changes" (D. Appleton & Co., 1889), Ch. IX. Wells, however, did not advocate a "planned economy." On the contrary his conclusion was that government restrictions of various kinds on the flow of trade should be eliminated. Incidentally Wells was an internationally recognized student of and authority on economics and was Special Commissioner of Internal Revenue under President Cleveland.

[2] David Friday, "The Probable Trend of Interest Rates" (The Annals of the American Academy of Political and Social Science, Philadelphia, Vol. 97, p. 33, Sept., 1921).

[3] Guy Tugwell, "Design for Government," Political Science Quarterly, Vol. 48, No. 3, September, 1933 (Academy, p. 325, of Political Science, New York).

As often as the proposition has been argued, so often has experience demonstrated the proposition to be wrong. Each time in man's experience since the industrial revolution depressions have been overcome by the investment of capital, the necessity for which the Socialists—the economic planners—have previously either denied or ignored.

Moreover, leaving aside for the moment the question which is uppermost in many minds—"Is there any new industry such as the automobile industry or the railroad industry which will employ sufficient capital and labor to lift us out of the depression?" —Leaving this question aside, there still remains unanswered by the advocates of Socialism or Communism or a planned economy the proposition of the necessity for capital investment to replace existing capital equipment. In a highly industrialized country capital wears out, machines deteriorate, become obsolete, and new ones must be substituted for them. Moreover, in a society in which the competitive forces control the price level, industries are constantly shifting, requiring not only capital investment for replacement in a new and cheaper locality, but also capital investment in residential and business buildings and in the countless additional human activities which are the concomitants of a new or expanding industrial center.

It can be safely stated as an axiom of the machine period that the greater the amount of mechanical appliances, the greater is the demand for capital to replace the obsolete and depreciated equipment.

Before the depression, the new capital annually

invested in the United States ranged between 20 and 35 billions of dollars, of which from 40 to 60 per cent was in replacement of obsolete and depreciated consumers' and producers' capital equipment.[1]

Since the beginning of the depression, with no confidence as to the future, few replacements have been made. There is therefore an enormous stored up demand on the part of industrialists, householders, every conceivable sort of enterprise, for the replacement of machinery which has long since efficiently served its purpose.[2] The advocates of Communism and Socialism, whether they call it "serviceability for vendability," a "planned economy," or whether they call it by some other equally pleasant phrase, therefore, have no grounds to stand on, either in experience or in fact—at least insofar as this point is concerned.

And now to revert to the question which was laid aside: "Is there any new industry such as the automobile industry or the railroad industry, requiring a sufficient employment of capital and of labor to lift us out of the depression?"

While the investment of capital for replacements alone is sufficient to reemploy a substantial part of the unemployed, nevertheless the question of new industries deserves some attention. The Communists

[1] National Bureau of Economic Research, Bulletin 52. "Gross Capital Formations in the United States."

[2] Variously estimated at from 28 to 85 billion dollars, probably somewhere in vicinity of 50 billion. Herve Schwedersky, "A Composite Estimate of the Theoretical Depression Backlog in Durable Goods." The Annalist, Vol. 45, No. 1152, Feb. 15, 1935 (The N. Y. *Times* Co., N. Y.).

or Socialists allege that there is no such new industry. This, it seems to me, is the philosophy of despair, for if there be no such industry then it makes little difference whether we cling to a capitalistic society or are transformed into a Socialistic or Communistic one—capital, whether invested by the State or by private enterprise, will not be made for productive purposes and employment will remain static. It is no argument for either the Socialist or Communist to state parrot-wise that there is no new industry for the employment of capital and labor. In essence, the statement is simply that there is no hope for the reemployment of people except by a thorough share-the-work program which must reduce the standard of living and distribute poverty.

The proposition itself rests upon the assumption that man has reached the limit of his capacity to harness natural resources for his own benefit. While many times before in history men, in ignorance of what they were believing, have held such views, every time they have been demonstrated to be wrong. At any one particular moment it is altogether probable that the average man cannot see a new great industry silhouetted against the horizon. This is but human. Yet, as one looks back over the past twenty-five years and recollects that within its span, man, by his own ingenuity, has been able to defeat the law of gravity; that he has invented and perfected the internal combustion engine with all of its manifold effects upon employment, distribution of income, mode of human living and measure of human happiness; that he has developed a thousand and one various articles which satisfy human wants—in the light of this brief survey, surely we cannot now, simply because we have broken temporarily the free flow of human initiative by the philosophy of despair, conclude that suddenly man's ingenuity, impelled by the profit motive, a few years ago so prolific, has now become completely sterile. I must concede that, were the Socialists and Commusists, the "serviceability-ites" to impose their doctrine, all hope of future progress might well be completely abandoned. Under such circumstances one may with reasonable certainty anticipate a completely static society—I should say a degenerate society—for anything which is static stagnates.

The second argument adduced in support of a Collective State—a planned economy—is that the machine denies employment. This, too, is not new. It has appeared in many previous depressions, during the Napoleonic War and post war depression, in 1811, and again in 1816 when General Ned Ludd, at the head of his ragged army, marched through Lancashire and other parts of England destroying the machine on the grounds that the machine denied employment.[1] Even today the proposition is generally accepted. It is probable that it is the basis of the proposed thirty-hour week law. If it is true, can the advocates of a Planned Economy answer this question: Why is it that during the course of the last hundred years, despite a mechanization theretofore considered fan-

[1] Hammond, J. L. & B., "The Skilled Labourer" (Longmans, Green & Co., London, 1919), Chs. IX, X, and XI.

tastic, despite more than a 100 per cent increase in population, up to 1928 there was practically no unemployment except those who because of old age or serious injury were incapable of working? If the proposition be correct that the machine does deny employment, then, in view of the amazing extent to which the machine has been applied to the production of goods and the extraordinary increase in population for more than a hundred years, we should have had a consistently mounting permanently unemployed population until in 1928, it should have numbered more than 20 million adults. This, however, was not confirmed by facts.[1]

A reduction in hours of work effected gradually is not sufficient to explain the discrepancy. It is interesting to observe that not so long ago Malthus

---

[1] Some may say that the failure of population to increase as rapidly as it had formerly increased and the disappearance of the frontier must have far reaching consequences on our economy. It seems to me that since the frontier did not disappear suddenly—as it were overnight—and since the rapidity with which our population increased did not at a given moment change, it is difficult to place too high a value on these two factors, particularly since other countries in Europe maintained a fair degree of prosperity in the face of no frontier at all and a diminishing population.

Moreover, the population of the world is still increasing with great rapidity. There are, therefore, throughout the world, markets of huge proportions if we will but seek them.

On the whole it seems to me that while the frontier with its undeveloped natural resources and its opportunity for economic independence has been of great significance in our economic history, one of its effects was to absorb the mal-effects of bad legislation, inflation and deflation, etc. The conclusion to be drawn is, as I view it, that to the extent to which it has disappeared, to the same extent we can no longer afford the extravagances in bad legislation which the frontier previously absorbed.

held the converse to be true, i.e., that man's ability to produce would not keep pace with the growth of population and that mankind would be faced with starvation. Within what a short span of years man's point of view has changed!

It seems to me that there is very good reason for our experience of increased mechanization, increased population and increased employment. I recognize the error of drawing a general conclusion from but a few specific cases. Yet a few cases in this instance are illustrative of a general principle.

It was not so long ago that in a Midwest town two men, obscure, unknown, of little means, invented an instrument no larger than a hat—the Delco self-starter. Its applicability to automobiles was soon demonstrated. Thereafter, its installation, instead of requiring human labor to whirl a crank, merely demanded, at first a foot pressed downwards upon a little lever, and now, the light pressure of a finger —even a baby's finger—on a button, to put into motion the internal combustion engine which provides the motive power for an automobile. This little instrument denied or diminished human labor in the specific act of starting a motor car. From it then unexpected but now rationalized effects flowed. The ability of man to start an engine without the physical exertion incident to the old necessity for cranking made the automobile an article which human beings desired to buy. Under highly competitive forces the automobile industry directed its energies to the production of an article at lower and lower prices so that more and more people could buy more and more automobiles. This in and of itself—to supply the steel, copper, lead, wood, lacquer, shellacs, bakelite, cotton and woolen fabrics, chromium, nickel, cobalt—required the employment of labor from the iron mines of the Mesabi Range, through the furnaces, the rolling mills, the lathes, the ballbearing plants, the machine tool factories, the chemical industries, the automobile plant—from the source of raw materials through the various processing operations to the finished article. The greater production of the motor car for more widespread consumption created a demand for roads—good roads—and the good roads made it possible for hundreds of thousands of people working in metropolitan areas to build and to maintain in the country their residences and homes, no matter how humble. These are but a few of the manifold labor-employing effects of the development of the little Delco self-starter which, insofar as the specific act of starting an automobile was concerned, diminished the amount of human effort required but which in its ultimate effects created perhaps a thousand, perhaps a hundred thousand times as great a demand for labor as the demand which it destroyed.

The case in point irrefutably exemplifies the principle that an invention of a new product to satisfy a new human want or a perfection of an article already in existence creates a multitude of new desires to be satisfied, new demands to be met and incommensurate additional opportunities for employment.

Or another instance—take as an example the matter of mining copper ores: Thirty years ago, probably four times as many men were required to break and mine a ton of ore as is now required, simply by reason of the installation of a machine drill. But is not the decrease in employment more than compensated for by the employment incident to the mining of the iron ore in the Mesabi Range; to the reduction of the iron ore into steel of which the machine drill is made; by the employment incident to the manufacture of the steel into not only the machine but into replacement parts for the machine; by the employment incident to the mining and reduction of iron ore into iron and its fabrication into the pipe to deliver air down the shaft, through the drifts, to the air drills; by the employment incident to the manufacture of the rubber hose to convey the air from the end of the iron pipe to the machine drill, and by the employment incident to the making of the power-generating equipment and the transmission of that power to the compressor, which forces the air down the shaft through the pipe, out through the drifts, through the rubber hose, to drive the machine drill?

The general principle which these two examples illustrate is that, whereas the application of a machine to one specific act may diminish the demand for labor in the performance of that act, the creation of the machine, both in its production and in the replacement of its spare parts, in the replacement of it, itself, as it wears out, and in the production of all of the many articles which the development of that machine creates, engenders a much greater demand for labor than the demand which it destroys; makes for more efficient production generally at lower prices, thereby stimulating a greater demand and a larger volume to satisfy that demand; develops a multitude of new wants and desires to be met by employment of additional labor in their production —and so on ad infinitum.

The Collectivist, the Planner, argue further that the development of the machine with its alleged tendency to concentrate means of production in great combinations has removed all opportunity for the individual to attain a position of economic independence. While it is probably true that the development and application of the machine to the production of goods for the satisfaction of man's wants has tended toward large scale production and, in many industries, concentration of the means of production, it is probably equally true that when concentration proceeds beyond a certain point inefficiency and higher costs replace efficiency and lower costs. Mere size, when it goes beyond certain limits, may contain in itself inherent elements of inefficiency arising out of the impossibility of any human mind or the coordination of a number of human minds to comprehend it. There is considerable evidence both in government and elsewhere to support this view. The test, however, can not be determined by legislative or executive dicta. The sole and exclusive test is competition. If size be inefficient, competitive forces, if permitted to operate, will destroy size, thus increasing the opportunity for individual initiative and economic independence.

Moreover, in a competitive society, it is not at all true that opportunities are not available to the able, competent, and industrious individual to attain a position of independence provided he is willing to accept the opportunities when they arise, provided he has the courage to search them out, provided he is willing to cherish the old virtue of saving. America, it is to be hoped, is still, and always will be, the land of opportunity for those who have the competence to make it so. Neither America nor any other country can be a land of opportunity for the incompetent, the coward, the sluggard.

But aside from this, if it be true that the machine has diminished the opportunity for economic independence, is it a valid argument for the Socialist, the Communist, the Planner, to advocate a system which destroys all opportunity for independence? Is not, at least, a diminished opportunity for independence better than no opportunity at all? For, as I attempt to point out later, the Collective State reduces man's status to that of an automaton.

And what is more—if, as the economic planner alleges, mere size is an evil, is it changing evil into virtue to increase size by transferring property to the State and converting the State into one gargantuan industrial enterprise?

But there are still others among the Collectivists who urged that "surplus value" created by labor is, under capitalism, diverted to savings or capital. As will, I think, be demonstrated, savings are necessary in any social or economic system. Thus, in a Collective State, surplus value is not distributed by transferring the title and operation of property to the State.

The aim, I suppose, of the Socialists, the Communists, the Planners—call them what you choose— is equality—not equality of suffrage for that has already been attained; not equality before the law for that is something which men already have—but equality of income, equality expressed in terms of possession of goods.

To attain the objective all property vested in individuals known as private property, whether it be farm land, life insurance policies, endowments, stock certificates or bonds, cattle, guinea hens or pigs, is to cease to exist as such and is to be covered into the State. Or, expressed in different terms, the State is to own and operate every conceivable kind of property and means of production.

There are many things about such a system which provoke thought. Those who advocate it conceive of the State as something more intelligent, endowed to a greater extent with wisdom, than are the individuals which are but its integral parts. Though doubtless they would not concede it to be true, they must believe that the State can do no wrong. This, it seems to me, is an illusion, for the State is composed of its integral parts, the individuals acting through their representatives. The State is therefore subject, at least, to all of the fallacies, errors, ignorances, prejudices and limitations, of those who compose it.

But the probabilities are that in the State there will be found more than merely the fallacies, errors, ignorances, of the average individual. For many years the positions in the government have gone to the political victors. For almost a century the standard of appointment has been, "To the victors belong the spoils." Very frequently it is with this knowledge that political organizations are maintained, and more frequently it is because of this knowledge and the hope of patronage that political organizations wage effective battle. Loyalty to a political party is almost always a condition precedent to appointment. Moreover, while it is not universally true, it is nevertheless not infrequently a fact that those seeking appointment are not always the ablest and most public spirited of our citizens. Of this we have, within our own experience, such an abundance of evidence that it can hardly be questioned.

It would be reasonable to expect, therefore, in the State a group of employees and administrators, political partisans, political workers, more frequently than otherwise the less efficient and able of our citizens.

But, in addition, I am constantly confronted with this query: If, in a democracy, representatives and executives with great difficulty have dealt with the relatively simple problems of political science, how can it be expected that they will be able to deal intelligently with the highly intricate technical matters involved in the production and the distribution of more than a half a million industrial as well as agricultural products?

To refer to but one of the many practical difficulties, let us assume under a democracy State ownership of all means of production. Can it be that the Congressmen standing for election in each district will refrain from promising their constituents the establishment of factories to produce shoes and hats, suits and coats, pajamas and collar buttons, tomato juice and can openers? And can it be that when elected they will refrain from log rolling and trading to satisfy the demands of their constituents? Can it be that they will not do what is now done in the matter of tariffs and veterans' hospitals, post offices and rivers and harbors projects, irrigation districts and mine experiment stations? Or, if the power to establish factories is delegated to an executive agency, will the Members of Congress, the National Committeemen, the representatives of labor and of the press, refrain from exerting the political pressure which they now exert?[1] To answer

[1] Charles A. Conant, "A History of Modern Banks of Issue" (G. P. Putnam's Sons, N. Y., 1908), pp. 333-4. In speaking of the Bank of the State of Alabama, incorporated under an Act passed December 21, 1820, the author says:

". . . The president and 12 directors were chosen by the General Assembly and the choice of directors for the branch banks increased the number annually chosen to between 60 and 70. Candidates for the assembly were compelled to promise their supporters liberal loans in case of election and to exact pledges from candidates for the directorships that the loans should be granted. One of the hotel keepers of Tuscaloosa succeeded in securing an election as director in 1832 and his hotel swarmed with members of the legislature and persons desiring to borrow money, who hoped to secure his support in the negotiation of loans. Four other hotel keepers realized that they were conducting business under a heavy handicap and secured their own election as directors in 1834. A director could not afford to refuse a discount requested by a member of the legislature and the discounts of the bank increased from $448,859 in 1826 to $20,642,473 in November, 1837. The circulation had swelled in the meantime from $273,507 to $6,676,050."

yes would be to expect more than experience teaches
or reason confirms.

Thus the State, in view of practical experience and
probable expectancy, is not an agency which can do
no wrong, but one capable of doing infinitely more
wrong than the individual under a liberal economy.

No—it is not reasonable to contemplate, in a
democracy, in a society dedicated to individual liberty, a State wisely and intelligently owning and
operating or even directing the means of production. It follows, it seems to me, that if a planned
economy is to be attempted—by that I mean a
Collective State, or one planned by a central
bureau or bureaus which is but one step removed
from Socialism or Communism—all of our cherished
liberties, freedom of speech, freedom of the press,
political freedom, our representative form of government, must be abandoned. Let us examine the
full consequences of the abandonment of democracy.
And here it should be noted that the mere continuance of the form of Democracy does not insure a
continuation of its substance.

It means, of course, the establishment of a dictatorship. And what is here said about a dictatorship of Socialism applies with equal force to a
dictatorship of Fascism for though the form may be
different one is as much a planned economy as is the
other. It is conceivable that under such a political
system the more capable individuals, or individuals
with more than average capacity, would be in charge
of the operations of production and distribution, so
that what appears to be true of State ownership of

all means of production under a democracy might not be true of State ownership and operation of all means of production under Authoritarian control. Moreover, concentration of power in a dictator would avoid Congressional interference. In view of the writings of the advocates of planned economy, the efforts of the State probably would be focused upon increasing the distribution of consumers' goods, or, stated another way, upon increasing the amount of goods which each individual would have to enjoy. The emphasis thus placed by the economic planners is due to their failure to take into consideration the necessity for capital investment, or savings, in a highly mechanized age. They must assume mechanization at least at its present level, otherwise they must be willing to destroy the machine and revert to a completely rural and agricultural economy, thus leaving forever stranded upon society many millions of pauperized individuals.

As has been pointed out elsewhere, machines wear out. They do not last forever. The buildings in which machines are housed depreciate and deteriorate. Houses in which people live require repairs. The whole vast economy built upon power and the ingenuity of man to convert natural resources and the powers of nature into instruments of production is one which is constantly shifting, never static, requiring investment of capital to replace worn out and broken parts. Moreover, in addition to the capital required for replacements, there may be, even under a Dictatorship, some new enterprises to be developed, requiring the investment of capital, but of this more anon for there exist serious and real grounds for doubting the possibility of progress under an Authoritarian State. And so, for the moment, the question of capital for new ventures will be set aside for discussion later.

But among those who have an understanding of the machine age there can be no doubt of the necessity for capital investment, which is another way of saying savings or surplus value, for the purpose of making replacements even under a Dictatorship. The emphasis placed upon the distribution of goods, i.e., consumption goods, overlooks this requirement. If, however, the economic planners recognize its necessity, as some of them both in this country and in Russia are giving some evidence of doing, then under an Authoritarian State how is this division between consumption and capital goods, between distribution and savings, to be made? And if there is to be a division, how much is to be reserved from income for savings for capital investment, and how much is to be distributed in consumers' goods? What is the test in a vast economy involving the production of hundreds of thousands of articles, the operation of hundreds of thousands of plants, the tilling of many millions of acres with hundreds of thousands of plow shares, harrows? How much is to be reserved? What is the measure which the Authoritarian State will apply? If too little is reserved, then the cost of production must go up because of the greater inefficiency of its plants incident to failure to replace, thus increasing prices, or if there be no prices, diminishing the amount of goods to be distributed. If, on the other hand, the Authoritarian State reserves too much for investment, then again prices must be higher than they would otherwise be, because industry will be over-capitalized, and again the consumer is injured. Thus, whether it be too little or whether it be too much savings which are reserved by this omniscient, omnipotent State, the consumer always suffers.[1]

It seems, therefore, that not only is it impossible in a planned economy to measure the amount of production which should be reserved in the form of savings for capital investment, but also that if savings are made, they must come, just as they always in the past have come and always in the future must come, directly or indirectly out of production, thus, diminishing the *present* distribution of products among the people. But the most important consideration is that while, in the liberal economy under a proper banking system, the automatic forces control the amount and disposition of savings, in a planned economy those automatic forces no longer exist. No test or measure of the savings required has been suggested except the loose, meaningless measure of "social welfare" which the dictator must make meaningful.

With respect to the matter of distribution of goods under an Authoritarian State equally grave questions arise. Imagine, if you are able, State ownership of every conceivable industrial, commercial and agricultural activity in the United States, stretching

[1] This is clearly evidenced by the Russian experiment.

from the Atlantic to the Pacific, and from the Canadian line to the Mexican border. The free forces existent under a Liberal Economy—demand and supply—have been destroyed. The State is the sole producer and the sole distributor. Some of the primitive "economic planners" advocate a mere distribution of goods—destruction of the money system. This involves the complete annihilation of the geographical division of labor and a complete resurrection of the system of barter. But more than this, it means that the number of shoes shipped to Keokuk, Iowa, would be dictated by the State, and that each individual would be required to take so many shoes, quite irrespective of whether he might want shoes or whether he would prefer to have perhaps a necktie, or two neckties in lieu of the required number of pairs of shoes, or perhaps a fishing rod instead of a pair of shoes. But under the Authoritarian State, the powerful and omnipotent voice of the State must say, "No, you must take so many pairs of shoes and you must like it." The whole nation must be placed on rations dictated by the State and must be clothed, fed and possibly housed, just as are the enlisted men in the army and the navy.

In the matter of distribution then, based upon mere exchange of commodities, the State must compel every individual residing within it to take so much and no more of the commodities which the State produces. It cannot permit a choice; it cannot permit of any freedom of taste. The citizens under the Authoritarian State must become as much alike one another as the penguins in Penguin Land.

In Soviet Russia it has long since been recognized
that the initial attempt to distribute goods without
a medium of exchange, a money, was completely
futile and impossible. Russia attempted a sort of
labor certificate as a medium of exchange. This ex-
pedient failed and now reluctantly the Authoritarian
State of Russia has come to the conclusion that there
must be a money and prices.[1] What would be the
kind of a system which would exist under a planned
economy with money and prices? The State, of

[1] "Money, Prices and Gold in the Soviet Union." School of
Slavonic and East European Studies in the University of London.
Monograph No. 3, Nov., 1934.
P. 3, 5, 6. "There is much evidence to show that in the period of
War Communism a policy was persistently pursued with the avowed
object of bringing about the ultimate abolition of money. The
National Economy Congress, which met at the end of December, 1918,
passed the following resolution:
" 'The social reconstruction of economic life requires the abandonment of capitalistic relations in production, and the ultimate elimi-
nation of any and every influence of money. The uprooting of
private financial enterprise, and the concentration of fundamental
branches of production and of distributive functions in the hands
of the State, offer sufficient grounds for the systematic disestablish-
ment of the monetary circulation.' "
"The programme adopted at the VII Congress of the Communist
Party, held in March, 1918, contained this passage: 'Basing itself
on the nationalization of banks, the Russian Communist Party aims
at carrying through a number of measures which shall extend the
sphere of moneyless settlements and prepare the ground for the abolition of money . . .' "
"On January 26, 1921, the Council of People's Commissaries issued
a decree setting forth that '. . . (3) Work must be begun without
delay to determine a unit of account or of values which will best
correspond to the labour organization of society and to the idea of
a budget in kind reflecting true economic transactions.' . . . The
ultimate outcome of the investigation was tersely summed up by
Professor Yurovsky of the People's Commissariat of Finance in the
following passage: 'Without entering here into the question as to
whether the problem generally admitted of a solution, we may say
that the extensive labour expended upon it produced no scheme
capable of practicable fulfillment, nor indeed any positive results
even of academic interest.' "

course, would be compelled to take in as much money as was required to pay its employees, to purchase from other State agencies raw materials, to buy from still other State agencies motive power or the wherewithal to generate motive power, to purchase foreign exchange with which to pay for its imports, in short to pay all of its expenses and to provide some sort of capital for replacement. Moreover, it is alleged with great confidence that the State would operate all of the plants now lying idle. Many of these had become obsolete even in the boom days by reason of their inability to produce in competition with their more efficient competitors. Thus, the State, operating all plants, would be compelled to fix a price level sufficient to permit the most inefficient of the plants to survive. Consequently real wages would be lower because prices would be higher.

Furthermore, what has been said about the regimentation of distribution of goods without money applies with equal force when money is used. The State being the sole and exclusive producer of all goods—no individual being permitted to undertake the venture of producing something which he thinks human beings may want, different, perhaps, from things already produced, different in shape perhaps, different in color, different in quality—the State must compel its citizens to take and pay for whatever the State produces. Practically all freedom with respect to individual tastes would be destroyed. Almost all selective inclinations of man must disappear.

And now consider the question of new enterprises:

Doubtlessly the advocate of Collectivism will point to the great philosophers and the great artists who, in the cloistered quietness of a monastery or a convent have produced great thoughts and works of great beauty for the education and entertainment of mankind. Doubtlessly they will refer to the scientist who, without thought of gain, plods brilliantly away in some college laboratory. There are some such, but they represent but a small fraction of the population of the world. Moreover, insofar as the practical application of a scientific invention is concerned, what test other than the profit or loss test can be applied to it? Given State ownership, bureaucratic operation of all means of production, what "yard stick" can be applied to the practicability of an invention, what urge will there be to risk a loss in the determination of the utility of a new discovery?

It has been the incentive of profit which in many instances has induced capital (although perhaps different capital), decade after decade, actually to sustain losses in the hope that in spite of experience of past failures a problem might still be solved. At last, in many cases, the hope has been realized and a new method of satisfying a human want has been produced, greater employment has been created, and the standard of living raised.

For many years failure crowned the efforts of those who first attempted to develop the steam engine on rails, and for many years disappointment pursued those who attempted to apply the internal

combustion engine to a vehicle. Would the State
have sustained years of consecutive losses? Would
the State have "saved" for the ventures?

Would we now have the automobile industry had
we lived in a planned economy? This is, of course,
a matter of opinion, but I would venture the definite
answer that we would not.

Under an Authoritarian State, what incentive, if
any, would there be for the production of new things
to satisfy new human wants? The urge of man since
the dawn of history has been to acquire greater satisfaction of his wants, to explore the unknown things
lying beyond the horizon, and it has been the incentive of profit which has induced the exploration.
It was the incentive of profit which led to the application of the inventions of Watt and of Faraday,
of Ohm and of Bessemer, of Edison and of Marconi,
to the production of things to satisfy potential
human desires. And it has been past savings which
in part have made the ventures possible. What motive would be substituted for the profit motive?

Some may proudly point to the operations of the
Post Office Department under government ownership and to the improvements which have been made
in the delivery of mail. It was not, however, the
Post Office Department which invented and applied
the improvements. The Post Office Department
merely simulated improvements conceived, attempted and found to be successful by those operating privately owned enterprises.

Some may point to the things which Russia has
done, but here again Russia has invented nothing
new, has applied nothing new, has produced nothing

new. Russia has merely been imitating the things which capitalistic countries had already demonstrated to be successful. She has even employed many of the great engineers made great under a capitalistic system to do for her what she could not have done herself. Given a planned economy, an Authoritarian State, without the example of a capitalistic order to follow, what progress can there be expected in the development and production of new things to satisfy new wants, or what incentive will there be to perfect, to make more efficient the production of things which it has already been demonstrated man desires?

Will the State be willing to take a substantial loss? Hardly! For in the absence of a measure of savings of capital to be invested, how can the State run the risk of loss unless it resort to the printing presses for the generation of its capital, and if it do this then it must destroy the purchasing power of its employees. Thus, under a Collective government the reasonable expectancy is a static society, and therefore a stagnant society, all hope of future progress gone, all thought of development destroyed, a completely dictatorial, tyrannical instrumentality, even more dictatorial than the monarchies which democracies have destroyed.

Not only will all freedom with respect to taste have been prevented, but all freedom with respect to the nature of a man's occupation will disappear, for just as the State must compel the distribution of goods, so must it compel the distribution of labor. But more than all of this, society and production having been made static, production having been

controlled, the State must then control consumption
for there can be no control of the one without control
of the other. The impingements upon human lives
of regimentation of production and of consumption,
are profound. One of the factors relevant to consumption is population. Therefore the Authoritarian State under certain circumstances must dictate how many of its employees may marry, which
ones of its employees may marry, if any, and if they
may marry, how many children, if any, each couple
may have.

The family, or at least family life, as an institu-
tion of a free state must be destroyed for it is a
breeding place of loyalties other than to the government. The church, too, must be abolished for it is
the meeting place for those with a faith in a god
other than the State; and there can be none other
gods but the State.[1]

[1] Will Durant, "The Tragedy of Russia" (Simon & Schuster,
N. Y., 1933).

Page 75—"The thorough-going Communist has of necessity declared war upon the family and the home; he knows that these are the
richest sources and the most persistent nests of those individualistic
impulses which must be destroyed if communism is to survive. Therefore he attacks the family relentlessly, by providing institutions for
the communal care of children, by strengthening the young against
parental authority, by putting an end to Sunday and to religion, by
encouraging restaurants, communal kitchens and "kitchen factories" (where prepared meals may be bought and taken away), and
by herding the peasants into collectives and the workers into clubs.
Home life is made almost impossible by overcrowding. . . .

Page 76—"The Soviet hope that by 1933 all its citizens will eat in
communal kitchens; but the people obdurately prefer, as yet, their
little share of the kitchen stove, or the smelly kerosene *primus* in their
corners, and the modest meals that they can cook by themselves according to their shamefully individual tastes."

(The above was written by Mr. Durant after his visit to Russia
in the summer of 1932.)

And, of course, it goes without saying that no employee (and all are employees), no citizen, will be permitted by the State to express a view inconsistent with its philosophy for this might lead to its destruction. The "Ogpu" will be prying into the utterances of every individual, of every human being old enough to speak the English language. Moreover, aside from theoretical considerations, the occurrences in Italy, Germany and Russia under various types of dictatorships make it difficult to escape the conclusion that a fair trial before one's peers under a Totalitarian State becomes a mere myth.

So the argument for equality, having moved on from political equality, equality before the law, to equality of goods, finally is silhouetted in the form of possible equality of goods, with everybody having less goods than they now have, but with not a vestige of equality either in politics, in the courts, or in any field of human endeavor. Moreover, the very existence of a planned economy assumes—as has been heretofore pointed out—an aristocracy of power—an aristocracy of planners who by reason of their position as a part of the dictatorial planning mechanism will be enjoying the perquisites of their office—perquisites which others do not enjoy.

It is, I think, of sufficient importance to point out that even in a Collective State, the budget must be balanced to prevent a destruction of currency, that wages must be controlled by the necessity to operate without loss, if not for a profit out of which savings for capital investment can be made.

Moreover, unless the State elects to pursue a

course of economic isolation, with its many unfortunate effects on its currency and its people, trade barriers must be reduced and costs must be controlled by foreign competition.

In all, under a Collective system the State must perform all of the functions which individuals now perform. It must become the employer, the capitalist, the banker, the merchant. They do not disappear, they simply become a part of the State. Nor does their incorporation in the State eliminate the evils now complained of. All that happens, aside, of course, from the social, political and human considerations, is that the State assumes the functions of individuals and operates under the same forces which exist under the present order.

Thus the search for equality of goods without removing the things which many now criticize destroys not only itself, but every other equality which man has wrung from a resistant society. In short, under an Authoritarian State, every vestige of human liberty must disappear. The rights of man will be replaced by the diabolical and tyrannical rights of the State and of the aristocracy of power.

The Collectivist, however, may say that after a generation of Communism, after the public mind has been sufficiently educated, men will exert the same effort which they exerted under the profit system in the hope of attaining public acknowledgment of having been responsible for accomplishing more good than their fellowman. Conceivable. But should this idealistic point of view be attained among men there would still be no equality in the things for which men under such a State would then be striving, for some clearly would have accomplished more good than would others. But the Collectivist might say, ''Ah, but men will strive for the attainment of power for power if not for good.''

If this, then, is what man will strive for, certain ones will attain greater power than others. Thus there will in this instance, just as in all others, be no equality with respect to the things for which men strive. It, therefore, seems clear that the equality so loudly proclaimed to be attainable under a Collective system is not attained at all, and that whatever equality there may now be, equality before the law, equality in the ballot box, will have been destroyed, and moreover that, the system under which it is proclaimed equality will be attained, but under which all equality is destroyed will be one which lowers the general standard of living, prevents all progress, is completely unworkable in a highly mechanized society, and destroys every vestige of human liberty, even perhaps to the most minute act of a domestic or a private life.

What has been said with respect to the completely Authoritarian or ''planned'' economy is in most respects equally true with respect to the conception of the Socialistic State held by some modernists— one in which all means of production are owned by the holders of fixed income bearing certificates. For this means, just as in the other form, a fixation of wages by the State, a fixation of prices by the State, a fixation of return by the State, an arbitrary measure of savings by the State, a completely static form of society.

The N. R. A. Codes accomplish or will accomplish substantially the same results, for a large number of the codes operate to fix prices, prohibit the installation of more efficient methods of production, restrict production. And if they be continued they will mean regulation by government of wages and fixation of profit. Quite irrespective of the equity of complete regulation, if the industrialist undertakes to seek of the government a guaranteed profit there is much to be said for government intervention to fix that profit and otherwise to regulate. The system thus created becomes as static, as immobile, as a completely socialistic State and is subject to practically the same criticisms.

The railroads, within our own experience, offer a very good example. For many years the valuation of railroads has been regulated by law, the rates have been regulated by law, wages have been regulated by law. What have been the developments in railroads during the last quarter of a century? Until the competition of the buses, trucks and aviation became a force had there been any substantial improvement in transportation, had the cost of transportation been reduced, had employment on the railroads been increased, had better and cheaper service been provided? On the contrary, we witnessed the lamentable spectacle of an industry which had become completely static, of an industry which had developed no improvements, of an industry which, by reason of its very stationary nature had become practically bankrupt. But more than all of this, what has been here said on the nature of a planned economy has been demonstrated in other respects during the course of the last two years.

In the spring of 1933, great powers were delegated to the Executive, dictatorial powers limited in terms of time to be sure, but nevertheless powers which within the period of their life could be exclusively exercised. Under them the economic planners determined that they were to make cotton growers wealthier by requiring them to produce less.[1] For a while, and perhaps for a while longer, the people of the country may look upon this as a highly beneficial act, but what, so far, have been the consequences?

From our own experience it has, I think, been demonstrated that the restriction of the production of cotton has had profound effects upon the tonnage of traffic carried by trucks in the cotton growing States, in the employment of labor, in the shipping (outbound and inbound) in the Southern seaports, in the consumption of fuel by ships and railroads, in the employment of labor in all the manifold activities which are incident to the movement of the crop.

But more than this, the policy of restricting production which, mind you, was a policy determined upon by the economic planners, coupled with another policy of the economic planners, namely, fixation of the price of cotton, bids fair to destroy forever the export markets of the cotton farmer. More than 60% of the world production of cotton heretofore

[1] If a people can be made wealthier by producing less then a people should be made fabulously rich by producing nothing at all.

has been grown in the United States. The fixation of price, coupled with the restriction of production, has encouraged Brazil and other countries to increase their cotton acreage so that for the first time in almost a century the dominant position of the United States in the world cotton markets is threatened.[1] Coincidentally, I am informed that in England capital has been invested in different spindles designed to treat Indian and Brazilian cotton. The unmistakable result is that the Southern cotton farmer may permanently have lost at least a part of his market. If, however, he has not forever lost it, now that the acreage has been so substantially increased elsewhere in the world, he must confront a competition which he never before was compelled to confront. But, if, on the other hand, his market is gone, if his foreign market has been destroyed in perpetuity, then as a direct result of this act of the economic planners we must prepare ourselves for the deplorable reality of an almost completely pauperized Southern tier of States, extending from the Atlantic through and beyond the Panhandle of Texas.

But the economic planners have done something more. In order that the cotton farmer may be paid for the cotton which he does not produce, the economic planners have imposed upon the textile manufacturers a processing tax, thus increasing the cost of production of textiles. Not satisfied with this in-

[1] Cotton acreage in Brazil increased from an average for the years 1925-1930 of 1,264,583 acres to an estimated average of 2,613,000 acres for the years 1933-1934.

crease in cost of production, the economic planners have imposed an additional increase in costs of production through the Cotton Textile Code, with the result that not only is the cotton textile manufacurer no longer able to compete in foreign markets as he formerly did, but also he is not even able to compete with foreign importations in his own market. However much economic forces freely working over a period of time may tend to transfer our productive energies from cotton textiles to other enterprises, at least it cannot be successfully denied that insofar as cost of materials and cost of labor are concerned, the economic planners have placed the textile manufacturer in rigid, iron shackles and have made it completely impossible for him to meet the competitive forces which are throwing men out of employment and onto the relief rolls.

It is not surprising, therefore, to find that as a result of this endeavor of the Collectivists the cotton farmer is losing his export market while the textile manufacturer is losing both his foreign and his domestic markets. Cotton farmers are being thrust upon the relief rolls, textile mills are closing down and unemployment in the textile industry is increasing.

What a creditable record for the economic planners! What an accomplishment to commend planned economy to the American people!

What may be the future plan to cure the evils of the previous plan no one can now prophesy, but that there will be one is reasonably certain. One plan leads to another; a step in one direction leads but to one more. Few there are who have the courage to halt in their tracks and to retrace their steps, making a frank confession of error. The New York *Herald Tribune* of April 25th carried the story that in Washington serious consideration was being given to controlling exports completely; that while the exports of automobiles and aircraft had increased, the exports of cotton had fallen and that in order that cotton exports might be increased the government would compel reduction of automobile and aircraft exports, thus stimulating foreign demand for, or rather foreign ability to buy, more cotton.[1] There may be some question as to whether the result with respect to cotton would be had, but there can be no question that the results on employment in the automobile, steel, iron, electrical and other industries necessary to the production of automobiles would be disastrous.

Why concoct these elaborate and futile plans when a return to a liberal economy would, if too much damage has not already been done, restore to the cotton farmer his export market and to the textile manufacturer at least the free opportunity to regain both his export and domestic markets? Why not permit the cotton farmer to grow as much as possible, sell at a competitive price here and abroad, and why not remove the multitude of obstructions the N. R. A. has created and permit the textile manufacturer to retain both his foreign and domestic markets without reducing the export market of the automobile

[1] N. Y. *Herald Tribune,* April 25, 1935, p. 11, article by Theodore C. Wallen entitled ''Davis Suggests Car Export Cut to Help Farms.''

manufacturers? Why plan for poverty when, under a free economy, prosperity is attainable.

But we have another example—a planned money. Among the powers delegated to the Executive in the spring of 1933 there was the autocratic power to plan money. In this respect, how successful have the planners been? And these remarks are not limited to the acts of the economic planners within the United States, for other planning economists in other countries have been given substantially the same powers. Currencies, under the money planners, have become more chaotic than they have been in more than a century, and the chaos in planned money through depreciation, has added to the tariffs and the quotas an almost insuperable barrier to world trade. Thus the money planners have driven the world further in the direction of intense nationalism, have created greater economic pressures upon many economies and, therefore, have forced a greater use of the implements of economic warfare.

Intense nationalism—economic strife—can not long be waged with tariffs, quotas, exchange restrictions and—most powerful weapon of all—with depreciated currencies without running the risk of armed hostilities. But one is almost as destructive of human happiness as the other. The pain and suffering during the period of a war are great, but I doubt that they are more intense than the despair of the unsuccessful searcher for employment, the tragedy of the unemployed which economic warfare causes.

Another extraordinary example of the wisdom and

intelligence of the economic planners, another act which commends to the American people a planned economy!

There are many other examples, both cogent and impressive, of the impracticability of any group, under any sort of a system, successfully planning a whole economy.

There is one more, however, of such importance that it requires mention here. It is to be found, in addition to other provisions which vest in the Executive complete control over credit, in subsection (b) of Section 204, Title II, of the pending Banking Bill:[1]

This section, inserted at the instigation of the Governor of the Federal Reserve Board, reads:

"(o) It shall be the duty of the Federal Reserve Board to exercise such powers as it possesses in such manner as to promote conditions conducive to business stability and to mitigate by its influence unstabilizing fluctuations in the general level of production, trade, prices, and employment, so far as may be possible within the scope of monetary action and credit administration."

Expressly this language means a system of planned prices. Its implications, however, are much greater for under it the Federal Reserve Board is practically directed to control the activities of every industry and of every productive enterprise in the United States. It must be viewed not alone and as an isolated proposal, but in connection with the many other attempts to circumscribe our activities by gov-

[1] H.R. 7617, 74th Congress, 1st Session, Reported to the House on April 19, 1935.

ernmental dicta and to plan our economy.[1] In addition
it should be examined in the light of the existence of
many government owned Delaware corporations,
chartered under questionable authority, whose articles of incorporation contain the broadest of conceivable powers to undertake to perform every imag-
inable sort of human activity. Examined in its environment it fits perfectly with the program established by the Soviet Union and forms an integral
link in the chain of powers necessary to perfect a
planned economy. In the book, "Soviet Policy in
Public Finance," there is to be found reference to a
deadly parallel:[2]

"The credit system of the Soviet Union has developed considerably. The government has succeeded
in using one of the mightiest levers of the capitalistic
economic system in such a way as to make it serve a
socialistic organization. Though the banking tech-
nique of the Soviet Union and of the capitalistic

---

[1] Some of the many other attempts to plan our economy may be
listed as follows:

(1) The Agricultural Adjustment Administration Act and its clarifying amendments which vest in the Executive complete power to
plan agriculture and all processing of agricultural products.
(2) The National Recovery Administration which vests in the
Executive complete control of all industry and commerce.
(3) The Wagner Labor Bill which centralizes control of all employer-employee relations.
(4) The Guffey Coal Bill which, in effect, socializes coal mines.
(5) The Securities Act which, even as amended, tends to make the
United States Government the exclusive capitalist.
(6) The Social Security Act, immaturely considered, which tends
to socialize all savings.
[2] I. Reingold, "The New Economic Policy, 1921-1928," to be
found in "Soviet Policy in Public Finance," by Gregory Y. Sokolnikov & Associates (Stanford Univ. Press, Stanford University, Cali-
fornia, 1931), pp. 235-6.

countries coincides completely, there is a great divergence in their operating principles. The principle of preliminary planning, so characteristic of every branch of Soviet economy, penetrates banking as well. Credit, currency issues, and foreign exchange are handled by the banks in strict accordance with the plan laid down for the development of industry, trade, and agriculture, and with the general instructions received from the economic bureaus of the government.''

Even though, however, the section of the pending Banking Bill here quoted is not expressly for the purpose of presently controlling all industry, it nevertheless may make of the Federal Reserve Board the arbiter of the general types of industries to which credit may be extended, of the extent to which credit may be extended, and of the purposes for which credit may be granted.

Conceivably, it will submit the Federal Reserve Board to all manner of political pressure for the extension of credit of various kinds and in various different localities. And, since, under the Bill, the Federal Reserve Board and the system is made practically an instrumentality of the Treasury and of the Administration in power, it may well result in the granting or withholding of credit, not because it should be extended or withheld, but rather because political pressure dictates that it be extended or withheld.[1]

The case is strong against the planners. Experience proves that no group, however divine may be its spark of intelligence, is able successfully to plan the

---

[1] Probably the Eccles Banking Bill can best be defined as a bill to socalize bank deposits.

various activities of man engaged in hundreds of thousands of different fields and employed in the production of hundreds of thousands of articles which go to make up our complicated modern social and economic organism.

Moreover, both evidence and experience indicate that, however unsuccessful the present planned economy may be, it rests upon autocratic State control.

It denies in many industries the right to attempt to produce for the benefit of mankind at lower prices; in many it denies the right to produce at all; in many it penalizes for producing more than a given quantity; it denies the right to make adjustments necessary to maintain employment. It verges, then, upon the Authoritarian, tyrannical State. It lies in that shadowy field between Socialism on the one hand and Fascism on the other.

But the agencies of the planner can not remain as they are today for the search by men for power seldom ceases. The restless, irresistible urge is for more and more. We have much evidence of this in government in the lamentable fact that bureaus once created never are abolished and that bureaucrats once appointed are ever seeking broader fields of control. So must it be with the recent agencies of control and so, as a matter of fact, it has been.

At first, through Reconstruction Finance Corporation loans, semi-control of banking institutions was effected; now through a banking bill complete control not only of the banking system but of all our industrial and agricultural activities is to be attempted. At first the Agricultural Adjustment

Administration's control of agriculture was voluntary, then by a queer twist made compulsory, and now, under the guise of "clarification" there is sought complete control—autocratic control—not only of agriculture but of all processing industries. Not satisfied, however, with this large measure of power, all industry is placed in a straitjacket under the N. R. A. And even this is not enough to satisfy the lust for power. All labor must be subjected to the rule of the bureaucrats. And now the power to spend without Congressional interference, with its direct control over geographical areas, separate groups and Congressional personnel, has been attained. This is perhaps the greatest power of all and it has been so recognized, for throughout history there is recorded the constant struggle between the people and the State to control the purse strings. The urge for power never halts—it moves constantly onward toward more and greater authority. And so now the search creeps on apace. But even though there were no restless desire for the acquisition of greater authority, the confusion created by the effect of plans in one field of human endeavor running counter to the plans in another—the extent to which a plan in one segment of enterprise nullifies a plan for another segment—give rise to a demand for further and further plans. And so the plans lead on to other plans—the initial powers necessary to them give rise to further powers—the initial act of quasi-planning by reason of its inherent contradictions and confusion generates the demand for further authority, thereby making inevitable, unless checked by strong resistance—by a faith in the old virtues—a completely powerful and tyrannical State. Whether Fascism or Socialism is to be the immediate end the future will decide. But if it be Fascism, then complete State ownership probably will follow, for Fascism is but an interlude.

Do we as Americans consciously choose to repudiate the things in life for which we have always stood? Do we elect to be beguiled by soft, seductive doctrines into following a course which ends only in the destruction of equality and of liberty?

III

Dictatorship and a Fiscal Policy

There have been discussed, in the previous lectures, the errors of the Post-War period, and the direction in which the efforts to attain a planned economy are carrying us.

Equally important, however, in its social and economic consequences, and adding momentum to the forces already created, is the matter of fiscal policy.

There co-exist in the Federal government two powers: the first is the power to appropriate and to expend money, and the second is the power to make money. Whenever the appropriation and expenditure of money continuously exceed the revenue from taxation, governments eventually go bankrupt. The bankruptcy of a government, however, is different from the bankruptcy of an individual. We all know, some of us from personal experience, some of us from the experiences of our friends, of our acquaintances, and some of us from observation—but from whatever source we may have gained our knowledge, we all know that whenever individuals become bankrupt their creditors intercede and become the possessors of their property. The individual, his family if he has one, his employees if he has had any, and if it be a corporation, the stockholders, are the exclusive sufferers.

The situation, however, is different when a government becomes bankrupt. It is different in that, in the case of the bankrupt government there is no power greater than or equal to itself which can become the possessor of its properties, of its wealth, and in that practically all of its wealth is not, strictly speaking, its own wealth, but the wealth of its citizens—that is, unless it be a Soviet or Socialist State. Governments, therefore, never file petitions in bankruptcy; they never announce to the public in so many express words that they are insolvent. Instead of doing what the private individual must do, they resort to the power which the private individual does not have, the power to make money. It is the money which they make without any regard to the production of goods or to past savings accumulated out of production, which they use to pay their bills.

The methods employed by bankrupt governments have been various. When coins circulated as the only medium of exchange they resorted to the policy of reducing their metallic content. When paper began to appear in lieu of coins the governments issued paper. When the central bank was created by governments to control credit, bankrupt governments sold to them their obligations for which they issued the paper. And now the most modern of all expedients is to compel the commercial banks to take government obligations, to set up on their books a credit against which the government may draw its check.

It is interesting to examine the effects of these various devices. History is full of examples of the results of excessive spending and of the compulsion which it creates for the debasement of currency. It was the excessive spending of Rome during the Punic Wars which compelled reduction of the metallic content of the Roman coin. It was the excessive spending incident to making almost sixty per cent of the population of the Roman Empire beneficiaries of a government and of a great public works program which compelled Diocletian to devalue the coin to one ninety-sixth of its previous value. But, since in those days barter was practiced to a greater extent than in more recent history, the crushing effect of the fiscal policy on the population was not so great. When, however, in more modern times, barter had become less prevalent and a medium of exchange had, because of the division of labor, become necessary to a more complicated society, the effects of the use of paper money became more disastrous.

On the Continent of Europe, the deficits of the Crown in the early eighteenth century, were the cause of a flood of paper money directed for the Crown by that temporary financial wizard, John Law. Prices rose and the suffering of the people was intense. Within less than a century, under the direction of the Constitutional Assembly, France again was subjected to the devastating effects of fiat money issued to meet government deficits. The proposal to issue assignats was opposed on the grounds that in substance the same thing had been attempted under the Crown and that it had left destruction in its wake. The advocates argued, however, that what had been done by the Crown with bad effects could be done by direction of the will of the people with good effects; that conditions had changed and that what had formerly been wrong under a monarchy was then right under a democracy. Paper was issued, and each succeeding month and year the emissions corresponded with the deficits until the entire population save perhaps a few cunning speculators had become impoverished. It is interesting to digress for a moment to note that the argument which has in the past so frequently been made is often heard today, namely, that a certain act undertaken by a certain group is bad, but the same act undertaken by a different group is good. The truth is that it makes little difference by whom an act is undertaken; the test of goodness or badness is the act itself.

It was charged, for example, not so long ago that the deficits under the Republican Administration were bad, but that the deficits now being incurred under the present Administration are good. It is the deficits which are bad, quite irrespective of under what administration they are incurred, just as in France in the eighteenth century it was the deficits and the emission of paper money which impoverished the people and which were bad, regardless of the particular group responsible for the acts.

But to return—in Russia in 1917, it was the government deficits encouraged by the revolutionists which compelled the emission of paper money which in turn impoverished the Russian population and made them more willing listeners than they otherwise would have been to the siren songs of the Marxists.

Within our own experience we have had many demonstrations of the evils of paper money. In many colonies paper was issued to pay the Colonial expenditures of the French and Indian Wars. Prices rose and intense suffering ensued.

The practice became so prevalent that Parliament in 1763 passed an Act, "to prevent paper bills of credit, hereafter to be issued in any of His Majesty's colonies or plantations in America, from being declared to be a legal tender in payment of money, and to prevent the legal tender of such bills as are now subsisting from being prolonged beyond the periods for calling in and sinking the same." [1]

In the days of the War of Independence the Continental Congress issued and appropriated moneys to pay for the cost of waging the War and again prices rose and suffering was intense. The value of the money issued fell until anything which was worthless was referred to as "not worth a Continental." [2]

[1] A. Barton Hepburn, "History of Currency in the United States," p. 12 (quotation from "Historical Sketches of the Paper Currency," by Henry Phillips, Jr.).

[2] Wm. M. Gouge, "The Fiscal History of Texas" (1852), Ch. XXXIII, p. 240.

"Peletiah Webster, in one of his essays published in 1790, says of the effects of paper currency issued during the War to pay for its conduct, 'We have suffered more from this cause than from every other cause of calamity. It has killed more men, pervaded and corrupted the choicest interests of our country more and done more injustice than even the arms and artifices of our enemies. It has polluted the equity of our laws; turned them into agencies of oppression and wrong; corrupted the justice of our public administration, de-

The Republic of Texas, within the short span of its existence as a sovereign nation, experienced practically all of the malevolent effects of a loose fiscal policy. The deficits it incurred were met by the emission of paper money known as "redbacks" secured, interestingly enough, just as in the French Revolution, by public land.[1]

During the Civil War the deficits created by war time expenditures finally, in February of 1862, compelled the issuance of paper money—the legal tender notes, or greenbacks. The inflation which ensued, the boom which followed, the suffering which it imposed and the long tedious painful depression in its wake, merely confirm all previous human experience with government deficits and the manufacture of money to meet them.

The use of the central bank as an instrumentality of accomplishing the same purpose as paper money has had equally devastating experiences. This, too, is not a new device. Governments with deficits have frequently sold their obligations to financial agencies

stroyed the fortunes of thousands of those who had most confidence in it; enervated the trade, husbandry and manufactures of our country, and gone far to destroy the morality of our people.' "

[1] Wm. M. Gouge, "The Fiscal History of Texas" (1852), pp. 13, 57, 146, 203, 231, 318.

"If paper issues could make a people rich the Texans would have been the most wealthy people in the Universe. They no doubt, however, like others in similar circumstances, attributed to want of circulating medium the evils they suffered from want of circulating capital. . . . What they suffered from this policy is sufficiently attested by a provision inserted in their State Constitution adopted August 27, 1845, which declares that 'in no case shall the Legislature have the power to issue "Treasury Warrants," "treasury notes," or paper of any description intended to circulate as money.' It is never without deep experience of the evils of paper issues that a people impose such restrictions upon the rulers.''

while the financial agencies have emitted the money. In France, under Necker, government deficits at first were absorbed in part by selling its obligations to the Caisse d' Escompte du Commerce—the forerunner of the Bank of France—while the Bank issued the currency.[1]

In our own history, there are many instances of the same type of procedure. The form may have been somewhat different but the substance was the same.[2] Many States, during the period from 1825-1840, became enamoured of State owned banks. With but three exceptions all were ghastly failures. Almost all resorted to the emission of paper money. In some instances it appears to be the case that in part the deluge of fiat money emerging from the State owned banks was caused by State deficits.

In more modern history it is apparently established that the complete destruction of the mark in Germany was accomplished by the emission by the Reichsbank of the currency to purchase government bonds. No currency seems to have been issued by the governments of either Germany, France, Italy, Belgium, or Austria. The borrowings of the respective governments caused by excessive spending were purchased by the central banks with the currency which they issued. The mark was wholly destroyed, the·French and Belgian franc, the Italian lira, were

---

[1] Chas. A. Conant, ''A History of Modern Banks of Issue'' (G. P. Putnam's Sons, N. Y., 1908), pp. 47-48.

[2] Conant's ''History of Modern Banks of Issue,'' page 332, contains a good description of this particular phase of our financial history.

partially destroyed, and the Austrian pfennig became almost completely worthless.

In all instances the human suffering was intense; laborers, pensioners, widows and orphans with small annuities or endowment funds, were partially or completely crushed by the experience. The methods here described are those with which the world has had ample experience. They involve either reduction of the metallic content of currencies or the issuance of paper money, in the first instance by governments, and in the second instance by central banks. Wherever in the world men can be found who have lived through these experiences there is a revulsion to their repetition, for the social consequences have been great, the human suffering has been intense, and in some instances entire populations have been impoverished.

The newest of methods is for the government to sell its obligations to commercial banks, to receive on the books of those banks a deposit credit, to draw its check against its account for the payment of its bills, while the check circulates back into the same bank or a different bank. The ultimate effect is that bank deposits are increased. In a country in which 90 per cent of the business is done on credit, in which currency is not used to any great extent, but in which checks are used for the payment of obligations and for the transaction of business, the artificial creation of bank deposits by forcing government obligations —government bonds—upon commercial banks, is little different from the printing of money either by the government itself or by the central bank. If this be true, if there is in fact little difference between building up bank deposits by government fiat and government borrowing on the one hand, and printing paper money on the other, then the first is just as inflationary as the second, and the effects of the first may eventually be just as devastating as experience has demonstrated the second to be.

When government deficits are absorbed by the issuance of bonds purchased out of savings, no increase in the total volume of money or credit is effected, but when government deficits are met by the sale of obligations to a central bank and the emission of currency therefor by that bank, or by the emission of currency directly by the government, or by forcing upon the commercial banks government obligations, thus increasing bank deposits, there is in all instances a net increase in the total amount of money and of credit available.

Now, let us see in exactly what position we in the United States are.

In passing judgment upon our spending policy, it is important to view it in its setting—in the environment in which it exists. It is necessary, therefore, to enumerate the policies and acts which are tangent to huge deficits continuously incurred.

First, we find an Administration definitely committed time after time to a policy of raising prices by monetary manipulation. Second, we find the verbal commitment confirmed by specific acts. Among these have been the silver policy of the Administration, the gold policy of the Administration; an Administration which has demonstrated since the first few months of its existence curious and amazing ability to yield either in whole or in part to almost all inflationary pressures or proposals; and finally, what is probably more significant than any of the others save possibly the avowed inflationary policy, is the Banking Bill.[1] While there may be, although my own thoughts are not yet crystallized, some of its features which should commend approval, one of its basic purposes, however much it may be denied, is to guarantee the financing of a great spending program without the direct emission of currency by the Government itself. This is evidenced by an article in the New York *Times* of Nov. 25, 1934,[2] and by a news item in the New York *Herald Tribune* written by Ernest K. Lindley on December 2, 1934,[3] and is made conclusive by the evidence of the Governor of the Federal Reserve Board in his testimony before the House Committee on Banking and Currency while hearings were being held on the Banking Bill.

[1] The Eccles Banking Bill of 1935, i.e., H.R. 5357.

[2] Frank L. Kluckholm, ''Eccles Discusses the Tasks Ahead,'' N. Y. *Times,* Nov. 25, 1934, Section 8, p. 2, Col. 1.

[3] Ernest K. Lindley, New York *Herald Tribune,* Dec. 2, 1934, p. 1, col. 5.

''. . . The conviction has spread through most of the administration that the government should seek from the coming Congress sufficient control of the Federal Reserve System to assure that the government's borrowing and refinancing program will meet no obstruction. . . . A greater degree of control . . . is regarded in the administration as all the more important in view of the turn toward a policy of larger expenditures for public works. . . . The present indications are that the administration will adhere . . . to financing public works and similar enterprises by selling interest-bearing bonds, but with sufficient control of the Federal Reserve System to guarantee that the financing program cannot be blocked by a 'bankers' strike.' ''

The latter is most illuminating. Excerpts follow:

Congressman Gifford. . . . "You have no particular fear of a 40 billion dollar national debt in this country?"

Governor Eccles. . . . "I have no fear of a 40 billion dollar national debt."[1]

Governor Eccles. . . . "Inflation can only be brought about by the willingness of the people and corporations to borrow money, and that is one thing we are trying to get; we are trying to induce the borrowing and lending of money upon which recovery is based. We are talking about the fear of inflation or reflation, when, as a matter of fact, that is what we want."[2]

Governor Eccles. . . . "I think it is very necessary that there be a very close relationship and liaison between the banking system and the administration in power; and I think that the Governor of the Federal Reserve Board is the channel through which that relationship should develop, in the interest of the banking business."

Congressman Hollister. . . . "Can you not conceive of a situation where political exigencies might be in direct conflict with wise banking policy and wise credit policy?"

Governor Eccles. . . . "All I can say is that, if you have such exigencies—war is a case in point and

[1] Hearings Before the Committee on Banking and Currency, House of Representatives, 74th Congress, 1st Session, on H.R. 5357, p. 277.

[2] Hearings Before the Committee on Banking and Currency, House of Representatives, 74th Congress, 1st Session, on H.R. 5357, p. 299.

depression is a case in point—then I think it would be very unfortunate if the administration was unable to carry out its program. I stated, I think, when I first testified, that the responsibility of any administration in power is largely a social and an economic one. Practically all political questions relate to social and economic problems. An administration cannot be charged, when it comes into power, with dealing with those problems separately, free, apart, and divorced from the money system." [1]

Governor Eccles. . . . "I think it would be extremely unfortunate for the bankers if a situation was reached where the Government, having a continuous budgetary deficit, was unable to get the cooperation and support necessary from the Reserve banks and the bankers; for the reason that it would probably mean, under those circumstances, the issuance of currency rather than bonds to pay for the budgetary deficits. It would mean the possibility of the Government taking over the banking system." [2]

With this environment in mind an examination of government finances of the last few years and of the proposed fiscal policy for the next two or three years throws light on our present position and on the direction in which we are headed. Since 1931 the direct deficits experienced and prognosticated by the various budgets are as follows:

---

[1] Hearings Before the Committee on Banking and Currency, House of Representatives, 74th Congress, 1st Session, on H.R. 5357, p. 363.

[2] Hearings Before the Committee on Banking and Currency, House of Representatives, 74th Congress, 1st Session, on H.R. 5357, p. 372.

DIRECT FEDERAL DEFICITS
(In Millions of Dollars)

	Omitting Trust Funds
1931	$ 902
1932	3,148
1933	3,063
1934	3,989
1935	4,869 *
1936	4,529 *

* Budget Statement for 1936.

They were created since 1932 by three different general types of expenditures: Reconstruction Finance Corporation, Public Works Administration, and Relief Expenditures:

PART OF TOTAL DEFICIT ATTRIBUTABLE TO

Fiscal Year	R.F.C. Net Expenditures Exclusive of Relief	Public Works, Including T.V.A., Subsistence Homesteads and Emergency Housing	Relief from Appropriation and R.F.C. Grants Including C.C.C.	Total Public Works and Relief
1932	$767,735,209	$507,000,000	. . . .	$507,000,000
1933	978,964,464	474,000,000	$298,073,704 [1]	772,073,704
1934	1,274,353,652	656,262,924	1,844,424,580	2,500,687,504
1935	556,374,081	1,355,995,029	2,333,317,800	3,689,312,829
1936	Credit 112,263,675	4,340,800,150	None [2]	4,340,800,150

[1] Exclusive of $14,000,000 for C.C.C. and $34,000,000 for wheat and cotton distribution.

[2] The President, by House Resolution 117, has full discretion to use $4,880,000,000 of which $4,000,000,000 is a new appropriation and $880,000,000 is a reallocation of previous appropriations and grants for direct relief and public works. Most of it is to be used for public works. As of April 30, 1935, $150,000,000 has been allotted to F.E.R.A., $220,000,000 to C.C.C. and $3,630,000,000 of the new appropriation has not been allotted. It is interesting to note that expenditures for the months of February and March, 1935, decreased, but that during the month of April, after the passage of the $4,880,000,000 Relief Bill, expenditures increased very substantially.

This tabulation, taken from various budgets, and the Treasury Daily Statement, is interesting. It shows that a very large part of the deficit for the fiscal year 1932 was caused by R. F. C. expenditures. It shows that for the fiscal year 1933 about one-third of the deficit was accounted for by R. F. C. expenditures. It shows, likewise, that for the fiscal year 1934 about one-third of the deficit was caused by R. F. C. expenditures, and it shows that of the estimated deficit for the fiscal year 1935, less than 15 per cent will be accounted for by R. F. C. expenditures, and it shows that for the fiscal year 1936 no part of the deficit will be accounted for by R. F. C. deficits.

It discloses that, at the same time that deficits generally have been increasing and are estimated to continue to increase, R. F. C. expenditures have been diminishing and are estimated to continue to decrease, and that the expenditures for relief and public works have been increasing and are estimated to continue to increase. Or, stated another way, it discloses the fact that while the expenditures on which there may reasonably be expected to be at least a certain repayment into the Treasury have been diminishing—i.e., R. F. C. expenditures, etc.—the expenditures for which there will be no repayment at all have been increasing.

Expenditures for relief and public works create vested interests, while R. F. C. expenditures do not necessarily create vested interests in continued spending. So the point may be stated in still a different way: While the expenditures which do not necessarily create vested interests have been diminishing, the type of expenditure which creates vested interests and a continuation of spending has been increasing. This is an interesting and significant point, for it shows that, even granted the hollow recovery which we have had, expenditures for relief have not been diminishing, but on the contrary have been increasing.

An analysis of the expenditures for Public Works and of the reasons therefor is likewise interesting.

In 1933, approximately $474,000,000 was expended. In 1934, approximately $656,000,000 was expended. In 1935, there will be shown a substantial increase over the two previous fiscal years (estimate of $1,356,-000,000), while the budget estimate for the fiscal year 1936 shows a still further increase (estimate of $4,341,000,000).[1]

These are facts, not fancies. They demonstrate that appropriations and allocations for public works are not expended in the year in which appropriated or allocated, but are expended in subsequent years and that a public works program projects huge expenditures for many years into the future.

But there is another significant thing about public works. They were initiated on the theory that they would grant employment. This they have not done in sufficient amount to make any impression upon our own unemployment problem. The average employment during the fiscal year 1933, as a result of

[1] It is difficult if not impossible to make a segregation of this item, for the Budget for 1936 throws public works and relief expenditures into one category.

an expenditure of almost 500 million on public works was but approximately 350 thousand, both direct and indirect. The average employment during the three year period in which approximately $2,500,000,000 of the original $3,300,000,000 appropriated in June, 1933, was estimated to be spent, both direct and indirect was not in excess of 700 thousand annually, while during the month of December, 1934, the total employed by expenditures on public works was but 380 thousand.[1]

Congressman Louis Ludlow (Democrat), of Indiana, member of the Appropriation Committee, in an extension of his remarks before the House of Representatives, on January 24, 1935, said:

"When I asked recently how many persons had been put to work as a result of the $3,300,000,000 former Public Works program, the personnel director of the Public Works Administration gave the number as less than 900,000. At this rate it would require an expenditure of about $44,000,000,000 to give temporary synthetic employment to the 11,-000,000 persons now out of work. This, in my judgment, shows the absolute futility and utter hopelessness of the Public Works program as a means of solid national recovery."[2]

Congressman Ludlow seems to be correct.

The Administrator of Public Works, in a speech delivered before the Wharton School of Commerce, is reported to have said, concluding his speech:

"The real difficulty has been that not enough money has gone into the Federal P. W. A. program.

[1] U. S. Dept. Labor, Monthly Labor Review, January, 1935, p. 17.
[2] Congressional Record, Vol. 79, No. 16, January 24, 1935, p. 963.

You cannot do the work of fifteen billion dollars a year with three billion seven hundred million spread over 2 years. Some people either expected too much or they cannot forego even a poor opportunity to criticize.

"Lacking Divine power, the Administrator could not perform a loaves and fishes miracle. Fortunately, Congress has just made an appropriation for the continuation of the Public Works program. The country may be assured that we are not turning backwards. We are not even halting in our tracks. We are driving straight forward, our hands on the plow, following the furrow that we hope and believe will turn the soil for such a harvest as will add to the peace, prosperity, and happiness of the people."[1]

The statement is interesting and significant. First, it concedes that even with the terrific sum of money, almost $4,000,000,000, which was made available for public works before the $4,880,000,000 bill, employment granted has been insignificant when compared with our unemployment problem. Secondly, it confirms that which has been consistently maintained by the opponents of public works, namely, that expenditures undertaken for public works are ineffective relievers of unemployment unless the government take over all means of production, all the railroads, all the public utilities, every manufacturing plant, every building, every known method of producing commodities and in them make the investment for productive purposes which private capital would otherwise make if the Administration would but create the conditions under which private capital could seek

[1] Congressional Record, Vol. 79, No. 77, April 15, 1935, p. 5938.

investment with full knowledge that the only risk it was taking was the risk inherent in doing business. There is still another factor about the money expended upon public works: While the Administrator of the Public Works Administration refers with justifiable pride to the sale of $75,000,000 of municipal obligations, acquired by it in consideration for the loan of money for local public works projects,[1] the unfortunate fact remains that on December 31, 1934, there still remained $254,692,637 obligations of the municipalities which had not been sold despite the fact that unless the rules of the Public Works Administration have been changed they carry a rate of interest of 4 per cent, which is substantially higher than a rate for municipal borrowers of good standing.[2] Why have they not been sold?[3] Can it be that the loans are not sufficiently good to be saleable?

Under the Public Works Administration regulations, the rate of interest was originally fixed in order that the obligations of municipalities might be sold in the public markets so that, in the future, the municipalities and local political subdivisions would not be in a position to bring pressure on the Federal Administration to cancel their obligations.

This leads, then, to a legitimate query: If these obligations have not been sold to the public, how many of them ever will be repaid to the United

[1] Congressional Record, Vol. 79, No. 77, 74th Congress, 1st Session, April 15, 1935, p. 5938.

[2] National Industrial Conference Board (N. Y.)

[3] According to the Reconstruction Finance Corporation Statement of March 31, 1935, of the $75,010,401 obligations sold to it by the Public Works Administration, the R. F. C. has resold only $57,699,534

States? In view of previous experiences, would it not be reasonable to expect that those running for public office will pledge themselves to exert their effort to the end that the United States cancel the obligations of municipalities held by it and, therefore, may it not be that these advances will become direct obligations of the United States? Or, stated in another way, will these bonds. now held as assets, continue to be assets?

There is one other matter in connection with Public Works. The States, municipalities and local political subdivisions are now suffering from the weight of excessive debt contracted during the Post-War period and from heavy taxation incident to the debt thus incurred. In addition to this indebtedness all political subdivisions contracted, individuals and corporations, too, incurred a burden of debt excessively heavy, thus imposing upon them now a heavy burden to meet the interest and amortization requirements of their obligations.[1] It has been claimed and argued not without some justice, that the excessive debt so contracted was one of the contributing causes of the present depression. If this be true, how can it be argued with any justice, with any validity, that if excessive debt contributed to the causes of the depression, the depression can be cured by increasing the thing which contributed to its cause? How can it be argued that the tax burden in the political subdivisions can be diminished by increasing the obligations against the local taxpayers?

[1] Evans Clark, ''The Internal Debts.of the United States'' (The Macmillan Co., N. Y., 1933), Ch. I.

It is argued by some that Public Works constitute assets, that they are simply capital investments on which there will be a return. How many of them are so-called self-liquidating? How many of them in and of themselves create sufficient revenue directly or indirectly to pay for their cost; how many of them justify the incurment of additional debt to pay for them? At most, but a small number. On any score, therefore under present procedure except possibly that of reforming the physical appearance of the United States, Public Works, when not paid out of current income, cannot be justified.

Expenditures for relief, too, require analysis. They rose from $346,000,000 in the fiscal year 1933 to $1,844,000,000 in 1934, to an estimated $2,333,-000,000 in 1935 including the Civilians Conservation Corps, while the number of families on relief has risen from 3,850,000 in January, 1933, to 4,458,778 in December, 1934, with an estimated 4,540,000 families on relief in March, 1935.[1]

Some may attempt to explain this amazing increase in terms of reduced savings, increased standard of living for the unemployed, and therefore an increased per capita cost for those on relief, but whatever the explanation may be, the bald facts remain.

Moreover, the explanations attempted are not borne out by the experiences in Great Britain, which has been suffering from a depression for more than

[1] Monthly Report of the Federal Emergency Relief Administration, December 1, through December 31, 1934, p. 2. F. E. R. A. Release, April 28, 1935.

a decade. If the explanations offered were real, it would be reasonable to expect to find exactly the same conditions with respect to the increase in the

FAMILIES AND PERSONS RECEIVING EMERGENCY RELIEF
CONTINENTAL UNITED STATES

Year and Month	Resident Families and Persons Receiving Relief under the General Relief and Special Programs					Number of Transients Receiving Relief [3]
	Families	Single Persons [1]	Cases (Total Families and Single Persons)	Total Persons	Per cent of Total Population [2]	
1933						
January	[4] 3,850,000	(5)	(5)	(5)	•(5)	(5)
February	[4] 4,140,000	(5)	(5)	(5)	(5)	(5)
March	[4] 4,560,000	(5)	(5)	(5)	(5)	(5)
April	4,475,322	(5)	(5)	(5)	(5)	(5)
May	4,252,443	(5)	(5)	(5)	(5)	(5)
June	3,789,026	(5)	(5)	(5)	(5)	(5)
July	3,451,874	[4] 455,000	3,906,874	[4] 15,282,000	12	(5)
August	3,351,810	[4] 412,000	3,763,810	[4] 15,077,000	12	(5)
September	2,984,975	[4] 403,000	3,387,975	[4] 13,338,000	11	(5)
October	3,010,516	[4] 436,000	3,446,516	[4] 13,618,000	11	(5)
November	3,365,114	461,315	3,826,429	15,080,465	12	(5)
December	2,631,020	438,431	3,069,451	11,664,860	10	(5)
1934						
January	2,486,274	456,469	2,942,743	11,086,598	9	(5)
February	2,599,975	532,036	3,132,011	11,627,415	9	126,873
March	3,070,855	563,138	3,633,993	13,494,282	11	145,119
April	3,847,235	590,007	4,437,242	16,840,389	14	164,244
May	3,815,971	618,481	4,434,452	17,228,903	14	174,138
June	3,757,971	561,633	4,319,604	16,833,712	14	187,282
July	3,867,240	542,343	4,409,583	17,298,299	14	195,051
August	4,060,239	569,891	4,630,130	18,201,008	15	206,173
September	4,096,901	656,874	4,753,775	18,412,750	15	221,734
October	4,095,905	721,460	4,817,365	18,403,137	15	235,903
November	4,234,077	770,754	5,004,831	19,024,986	15	266,790
December	4,458,778	802,738	5,261,516	19,988,569	16	288,955

[1] Beginning with October, 1933, these figures include all teachers employed under the emergency educational program.
[2] Based on 1930 Census of Population.
[3] Middle of month figures.
[4] Partially estimated.
[5] Not available.

number on relief rolls in Great Britain. Yet this is
not the case. The number on relief rolls in Great
Britain has fallen.[1]

It is not unimportant to refer to a few other interesting facts in connection with relief expenditures.
The hearings before the Senate Committee on the
recent Works Relief Bill appropriating $4,880,-
000,000, page 102, show that 40 per cent of the 20
million persons on relief are in small villages and
on farms, and that only 12 million, or 60 per cent
are in the cities.[2]

Probably the large number in the small villages
and farms on relief can in part be accounted for by
the drought, by the A. A. A., by placing on relief
many who, during a certain part of the year, when
they are unable to work on their farms, are chroni-
cally without employment. Moreover, on the same
page of the hearings it is shown that 4 million of the
20 million on relief are Negroes.[3] But the hearings
do not show the allocation as between urban and
rural of the Negroes on relief.

It is frequently stated, though I do not know with
what supporting evidence, that in the agricultural
areas the relief policy has impaired in many instances and made impossible in others, the employment of sufficient labor properly to carry on the
operations of agriculture. But however this may
be, whatever the explanation, and whatever may be

[1] Great Britain. Ministry of Labor Report for 1934.
[2] Hearings before the Committee on Appropriations, U. S. Senate,
74th Congress, 1st Session, on H. J. Res. 117, p. 102.
[3] The total Negro population in the U. S. is about 12,000,000.

the ramifications upon agriculture and industry, the fact remains that the cost of relief has increased more than 600 per cent while the number on relief increased about 16 per cent between January, 1933, and December, 1934 [1] and this despite the claims of reemployment.

These analyses of the three general categories into which Federal expenditures have fallen are important because they demonstrate, at least in part, that the Administration, instead of holding expenditures down to an amount actually necessary, apparently has embarked upon a policy of spending just for the sake of spending. They are important, too, because they throw light, as shall be pointed out later, on the method by which the budget can be brought into balance without repudiating or denying the policy of adequately caring for the unemployed in our country.

So much for the expenditures which have been financed by the emission of direct obligations of the United States government. This, however, does not dispose of the financial policy of the Administration. Through the Farm Credit Administration and the Home Owners Loan Corporation, mortgages have been purchased by the issuance of bonds guaranteed by the United States Government. The total of these indirect obligations, actually issued, but exclusive of contracts to issue, exclusive of R. F. C. notes issued to banks for preferred stock, and exclusive of government guaranty of loans on home

[1] Monthly Report of the Federal Emergency Relief Administration, December 1, through December 31, 1934, p. 2.

modernizations, on November 30, 1934, amounted to:

Federal Farm Mortgage.....$	878,450,500
Home Owners Loan Corporation (Fully Guar.)........	1,695,398,425
Home Owners Loan Corporation (Int. Guar.).........	326,588,500
	$2,900,437,425 [1]

The total authorization is:

Federal Farm Mortgage ...	$2,000,000,000
Home Owners Loan Corporation	3,000,000,000
	$5,000,000,000 [2]

Congress has recently passed a bill increasing the authorized issue of the Home Owners Loan Corporation by 1¾ billions of dollars.[3] If this becomes a law, the indirect obligations of the United States will, therefore, be increased by this amount. It may well be that the mortgages held by the Farm Credit Administration will be paid off by the property owners. It may well be that the mortgages held by the H. O. L. C. will be paid off. It is reasonable, however, to expect—in fact there are already rumors which give grounds for the suspicion—that at some time these mortgages will be canceled and the in-

---

[1] Treasury Daily Statement, Nov. 30, 1934.

[2] Natl. Industrial Conf. Board Bulletin (N. Y.), Nov. 10, 1934. Vol. VIII, No. 11, ''The Contingent Debt of the Federal Government.''

[3] H. R. 6021, Passed House of Representatives March 12, 1935. Passed Senate in Amended Form April 12, 1935. Signed on May 28, 1935.

direct obligations of the United States government
will become direct obligations, at least in part.

Should there be an inflation with the inevitable
subsequent deflation, all of these indirect liabilities,
now sometimes referred to as assets—if they have
not by then become direct—will probably become
direct obligations of the federal Treasury.

Thus we find on the basis of this analysis that the
spending for the sake of spending has been increasing, that the portion of the deficits created by
unquestionably non-returnable expenditures has
been increasing, and that the contingent liabilities
are very great.

The question arises, how have these deficits been
financed? Have they been financed out of savings
or have they been financed by the creation of fiat
money or fiat credit? An examination discloses that
in the four-year period from June 30, 1930, to June
30, 1934, the Federal interest bearing debt increased
72 per cent. Holdings by banks of government obligations increased 190 per cent. Of the total increase
of $10,962 millions in Federal interest bearing debt,
no less than 77 per cent was accounted for by increased holdings of the banking system. Approximately three-fourths of the increase in Federal debt
in the four-year period ended June 30, 1934, was absorbed by the banking system.[1]

The deficits, therefore, have not been absorbed by
savings, but on the contrary, by fiat creation of
credit. At the same time that the banks have been

[1] National Industrial Conference Board, Memorandum No. 39.
''The Federal Debt and the Banks,'' p. 2. (N. Y., Feb. 13, 1935).

absorbing government obligations, bank deposits
have been increasing. Significant, too, is it to note
that bank loans and investments other than governments have been falling. This is evidenced graphi-
cally by the attached chart:

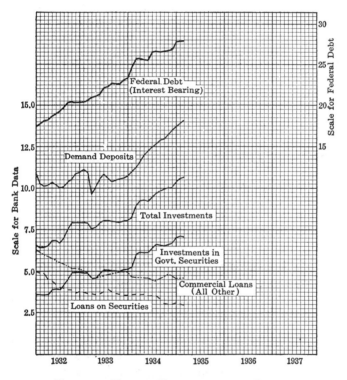

EFFECT OF FEDERAL FINANCING ON THE BANKS
(Bank date for weekly reporting Federal Reserve member banks)
(all data in billions of dollars)

This chart shows (1) how the Federal government is financing its
deficits and (2) what is happening to the money spent by the government.

The total investments of the weekly reporting member banks of
the Federal Reserve System constitute between 85% and 90% of

the investments of all banks in the United States. Although data for other banks, insurance companies and other such institutions are not currently available, the figures for the member banks reporting weekly are closely indicative of all financial institutions. Bank investments have been rising in approximately the same proportion as the public debt. Most of these investments consist of government securities, and the latter have increased more percentage-wise since March 1933 than either total investments or the public debt. This means that the banks are not only absorbing nearly all the increase in United States government securities, but they are tying up an increasing proportion of their assets in governmental debt.

Note that the rise in demand deposits since March 1933, has parallelled the rise in public debt and bank investments. Note also that there has been no increase in bank loans. What is happening then is that spendings of the government are returning to the banks in the form of deposits for which the banks have no use and which must be invested to pay expenses. Lack of borrowers and short supply of corporate bonds and notes have forced the banks to buy government securities. By causing an increase in demand deposits, unsupported by rising demand for business loans, the government is inflating the money supply as certainly as though they were issuing greenbacks.

While there may be some other causes for this situation, such, for example, as increased payrolls and the liquidation of debt, the fact remains that the increase in bank deposits almost exactly coincides with the amount of government bonds purchased by the banks.

While it has been true in almost all of our previous depressions that whenever deflation has run its course, rates of interest have fallen, there are in this instance several unusual factors. First, by attacking private enterprise, by encouraging disputes between employer and employee, by creating uncertainties as to the future, in short, by creating a set of conditions under which good borrowers are reluctant to use bank credit, the Administration has placed the banks in the position where, in order to meet overhead and taxes, the only investment which they can make is in government bonds.

Secondly, through Reconstruction Finance Corporation operations, the Government has placed itself in the position where it can coerce banks into purchasing government obligations.

Third, because among other things the Government has created conditions under which capital does not seek investment, and has by artificial methods pushed down the rate of interest.

Fourth, because the Government, both through the operations of the stabilization fund and the government corporations which have been created, purchases in the open market government bonds whenever they begin to depreciate, thereby giving to them a fictitious value.

Thus the level at which bonds are selling and their interest yield are artificial. The only true test of the credit of the government—a test not yet applied —is what savings are willing to pay for them.

Consequently we find that government deficits are increasing, that the Government has been financing its deficits by creating fiat money or its equivalent, that its credit is artificial, that there is no evidence of a determination to diminish spending. And we find, further, Administration support of a banking bill designed in part at least to assure artificial financing of future deficits.

On this point, the evidence of the Governor of the Federal Reserve Board, (to which I have already referred) before the House Committee on Banking and Currency is significant.

In the light of this analysis it cannot be doubted that we are headed toward inflation, that we have reached the point at which deficits are financed by fiat credit, and that at some time, just as in all previous experiences, we may reach the point where government deficits will be met by the direct or indirect governmental or central bank printing of fiat money. For even though the administration may oppose the emission of paper, the forces created by deliberate spending may force a currency inflation. But even if we do not, and, if present policies are continued, the time eventually will arrive when fear of bank deposits will induce an inflation just as it has arisen in all previous experiences with public fear of money.

Many great inflations have either been coexistent with or followed by revolutions. This is because the social consequences of inflation are almost beyond description. Intense suffering is experienced and the middle class is wholly or partially destroyed. Too much emphasis can not be placed on the importance of this great group of people with incomes— however derived—ranging from $1,000 to $5,000 a year. It is they who lend moral fibre to a nation; it is they who come to its defense; it is they who uphold its institutions; it is they who are its strength. Whereas the wealthy and the speculator may escape the destruction of inflation, the middle class has no means of defending itself and is invariably crucified on its cross.

It is, I think, true that France, having attained political equality, would have been saved the intense suffering, the mad fury of an impoverished people, the guillotine in the Place de la Concorde, had not her middle class been destroyed by the emission of assignats.

It is, I think, equally true that Hitler and Nazism would today be impossible in Germany had not Germany's middle class been destroyed by the post-war destruction of the mark. And it is conceded to be true by K. Shmelev, in "Soviet Policy in Public Finance," that the destruction of the ruble by budget deficits was a most effective weapon contributing to the success of the Russian Revolution.

"Toward the end of the civil war, when the system of military communism became clearly defined and further social development seemed to tend in the direction of complete naturalization of all economic relations, it was recognized that paper issues were not only a convenient method of financing the Revolution but also a handy way of combating the bourgeois regime because of the disorganization of money circulation which such issues produced. The booklet of F. Preobrazhensky, 'Paper Money during the Proletarian Dictatorship (State Publishing House, Moscow, 1920), will forever serve as a significant memorial of this mode of thinking. The author says in his preface (p. 4):

'I would like to dedicate this imperfect work of mine to the one who, by the perfection of his own work and by its unbounded abundance, gave me the impulse to write these pages. I refer to the printing press of the People's Commissariat of Finance. The revolutionary government of France managed to exist and to wage war thanks to paper issues; the "assignats" saved the Great French Revolution. The paper money of the Soviet Republic has supported the Soviet Government in its most difficult moments, when there was no possibility of paying for civil war out of direct tax receipts. Glory to the printing press! To be sure, its days are numbered now, but it has accomplished three-quarters of its task. In the archives of the great proletarian revolution, alongside the modern guns, rifles, and machine guns which mowed down the enemies of the proletariat, an honorary Place will be occupied by that machine-gun of the People's Commissariat of Finance which attacked the bourgeois regime in its rear—its monetary system—by converting the bourgeois economic law of money circulation into a *means of destruction of that same regime* (italics by K. Shmelev), and into a source of financing the revolution.' "[1]

Here, without attempting a comment and without drawing a conclusion, it is relevant to compare the various monetary, banking and fiscal acts of the Soviet in 1917 with those which have here been taken. The Soviet confiscated gold, obtained absolute control of the central bank, socialized bank deposits, directed their use in accordance with the Economic Plan, and finally, as has been shown, deliberately adopted a spending program both to finance the revolution and to destroy the currency. Here in this country gold has been confiscated, complete control of the Federal Reserve System has been obtained and is now being legalized, socialization of bank deposits and the direction of their use in accordance with a plan is demanded, and a policy of deliberate spending has been pursued.

In the light of a deliberate spending policy which,

[1] Gregory Y. Sokolnikov & Associates. "Soviet Policy in Public Finance" (Translated by Elena Varneck. Stanford Univ. Press, 1931), p. 111.

if not stopped, must certainly destroy our currency just as in all previous experiences continuous spending has destroyed a currency—in the light of references by Administration officials to the "New Economic Order," to the "Third Economy"—in the light of "We shall need no firing squads, no guillotines, no deportations or concentration camps"[1]— in the light of a policy of complete regimentation and an evidenced inclination to prosecute it, it is not strange that there are some who entertain suspicions with respect to the ultimate design. But whether there be a design or not is quite unimportant.

Almost 60 per cent of all outstanding direct government obligations are held by our banking institutions.[2] The Federal Reserve System holds 2.5 billions of government obligations.[3] Given a serious inflation induced by fear, given a depreciation of government bonds, we will be faced with the spectacle of a practically insolvent Federal Reserve System, an insolvent banking system, a Federal Deposit Insurance Corporation with its mechanism of insurance, i.e., government credit, wholly or partially lying in pieces, a destroyed middle class, an impoverished unemployed population and no government credit on which they can subsist.

[1] "The Progressive Tradition," by Rexford G. Tugwell, *The Atlantic* (Boston, Mass.), April, 1935.

[2] Natl. Indus. Conf. Board Memo. No. 39, "The Federal Debt and the Banks" (Feb. 13, 1935), p. 1, indicates 49.3% of all outstanding direct governmental obligations were held by banking institutions as of June 30, 1934. The proportion has unquestionably increased appreciably since June 30, 1934.

[3] Federal Reserve Statement of April 13, 1935, gave holdings as $2,430,000,000.

It is no argument to assert that the banks of Great Britain, in relation to their assets, hold relatively as many British government bonds as do ours. This may be true, but the point is that our banks hold the great part of our debt, that the public is not, therefore, buying government bonds, and that until the Budget is balanced, as it is in Great Britain, our banks, unlike the English banks, can not dispose of these government obligations without breaking the market and themselves. They must, therefore, hold them.

And so I repeat what I have said on other occasions, that the sheer weight of the economic and social forces created by a depreciation of government bonds will compel a dictatorship. It cannot be otherwise.

It is argued, however, that this can not happen in the United States. It is said that this can not happen here for we are too wealthy. In this connection it is not irrelevant to recollect that it was in 1862, when our national debt was less than $600 millions and when our wealth, undeveloped to be sure to the extent to which it has been developed since, was very great, that the credit of the Federal Government became obviously and apparently impaired, and that in order to finance the Civil War the government resorted to the infamous greenbacks.

Others argue that our per capita debt is approximately but one-third of that of Great Britain. The comparison, it seems to me, is irrelevant and immaterial. In the first place, in Great Britain the theory of taxation is that everyone who can possibly afford to do so must contribute something to the up-keep of the central government. For an unmarried man in the income tax brackets the exemption is $500 and the normal rate is 11¼ per cent on the first $875 of taxable income, and thereafter it jumps immediately to 22½ per cent. For a married man the exemption is $750, and the normal rates are the same as those for the unmarried man. But in the United States the exemption is $1,000 for an unmarried man, and for a married man the exemption is $2,500 and the normal rate is 4 per cent. Moreover, in Great Britain, largely as a result of this theory of taxation, out of a population of approximately 45,000,000, there are between 3,000,000 and 4,000,000 income taxpayers, whereas in the United States, out of a population of 125,000,000 or more, there are but about 1,900,000 Federal income taxpayers.[1] This is important for it evidences in Great Britain a political pressure against spending, which we so far do not have. But, in addition, there is in Great Britain a very definite fiscal policy. It is a policy, insofar as it is humanly possible and within the power of the government, to keep expenditures within income,

[1] These income tax rates prevailed in England until April 15th, 1935, at which time the Chancellor of the Exchequer introduced in the House of Commons a balanced Budget, with a provision for slight reductions. The new tax rates are as follows:

Exemption for an unmarried man apparently still the same, $500; exemption for a married man, increased from $750 to $850.

Tax on first $675 of taxable income, 7½%, instead of 11¼%.

Then the standard tax rate jumps to 22½% on taxable income over the first $675, whereas the old law levied a 22½% standard tax on taxable income over the first $875. (Pound sterling figured at $5.00. Information obtained from article in the New York *Herald Tribune* of April 16, 1935.)

whereas in the United States there is an equally definite, an equally fixed and an equally determined policy—a policy to widen the gap between expenditures and income to the greatest extent possible. So it is on these scores, on these particular points among others, that the comparison between the United States and Great Britain is not material; for the conditions are different. But more than that, to say that because Great Britain has a public debt three times as great as ours, we should proceed to contract exactly the same per capita debt, is very much like saying that because somebody else has scarlet fever we, too, should go out and contract it because it is a very good thing to have. Moreover, if a comparison is to be made it should be pointed out that the per capita tax in the United States is estimated to be $79.00, which is only slightly less than the approximate $91.00 per capita tax in Great Britain.[1]

A great public debt, even though a bearable one, is a menace, if for no other reason (and there are many other reasons) than that a great public debt impairs the ability of any country to finance itself in the event it is endangered by a hostile power, and places the government in the dilemma of either being destroyed by its armed enemies or deliberately imposing upon its people all the suffering and pain incident to a destroyed currency.

Still others argue that our great stock of gold is

[1] Per capita tax in Great Britain for year 1934-35, about $91.49 including local taxes. Per capita tax in U. S. for year 1934-35, about $79.00.

a steadying influence.[1] But, on the other hand, it is that stock of gold which lays the foundation for a certain type of inflation. Moreover, unless it be used, it constitutes no protection at all.

And, too, it is said that our favorable balance of payments is a protection. Possibly this is true, but our favorable balance of trade is growing smaller. Moreover, the balance can be converted into an unfavorable one when fear is really aroused. France, for example, had a favorable balance of trade during a part of her post-war inflation.

Others argue that because we spend to win a war we should spend to win a depression. In the first place, spending to win a war destroys a currency just as effectively as spending to win a depression. In the second place, when governments undertake to spend to win wars, there is more frequently than otherwise an automatic termination to the spending —the termination of the war. But when governments undertake to spend to win a depression, there is more frequently than otherwise an automatic continuation of the spending.

It is frequently argued that the ordinary budget is balanced and that borrowing for emergency purposes creates no hazards. Such an argument, to me, seems to be a fiction of romantic minds. The device of two budgets, an ordinary and an emergency budget, has been tried many times in history. All of the South American countries, or almost all of them, have attempted it. Many of the European countries at one time or another during their history

[1] Russia's gold stocks were about 1,250,000,000 rubles in 1917.

have attempted it, and always without exception it has resulted in the bankruptcy of the government which tried it. But more than that, and the reason for it is very clear, it makes no difference what governments borrow for—it is the process of continuous borrowing which finally compels them to resort to their power to make money, and it is the resort to that power which destroys the currency.

Others make the point that if we have a recovery the budget will be balanced. That argument, I think, is subject to very grave doubts. The Administration, under President Wilson, in 1919-20, collected the greatest amount of revenue that has ever been collected in our history. When industrial production was relatively high, when taxes were piled upon taxes, when the normal income tax rate was greater than the present normal rate, income amounted to approximately $6,600,000,000, almost twice our present normal revenue—approximately $2,500,-000,000 more than the maximum amount of revenue collected during the days of the New Era—of the American Mercantile System—of the "Boom." And yet we are told by the Administration that it contemplates spending at the rate of between $8,500,000,000 and $9,000,000,000. A minimum gap of between $2,000,000,000 and $2,500,000,000! Even assuming (a highly improbable assumption to make) that we will experience in the near future a recovery and industrial production and employment of people equal to that of 1919, how is the gap to be bridged?

"By diminishing expenditures" is the ordinary answer. But how many of the vested interests created by government spending (and vested interests can be created just as easily by spending as they can be by tariffs or by N. R. A. price-fixing provisions or any other one of the various methods of granting government subsidies)—how many of the vested interests so created will be willing to become divested? How many of the municipalities will be willing to take back to themselves burdens which they have pushed over on to the Federal government? How many of the retail merchants will be willing to see a diminution of government spending and consequent decrease in the volume of their business? Will the bureaucracy itself, created as a natural and inevitable concomitant of a great spending program, be willing without a great struggle to see itself dismembered? Will an Administration, which, by its acts and open statements, has espoused inflationary methods and huge deficits as instruments of recovery, have the courage to stop the spending and to convert the inflationary recovery into a deflation? An analysis of the course of the fiscal policy during the recovery which has been heralded and which in some measure we have experienced compels a negative answer.

In addition to all of this, the policy of spending creates inevitably increased permanent additional costs amounting to a good many hundreds of millions of dollars, expressed both in increased interest charges and in increased operating expenditures of the various departments. And of this there is some evidence already.

Finally, continued Public Works appropriations

pyramid contractual obligations of many hundreds of millions of dollars annually for many years into the future.

So that when one takes these things into consideration—the extent to which a bureaucracy already erected will not willingly and gladly see itself dismembered; the political improbability of an administration checking by retrenchment a hollow recovery which it induced by spending; and the record of increased spending despite a claimed partial improvement—it is highly improbable that under the present administration recovery alone will ever bring a budget such as ours into balance.

But there is another part of this argument which is susceptible of analysis. Can there be a substantial recovery with a budget unbalanced? Is government spending conducive to recovery? The great void in our national economy today is not in individual consuming power, it is not in the consumption of these things known as consumers' goods—it is in capital consuming power, and the consumption of things by capital. It is within the industries which depend upon capital investment that approximately 60 per cent of our unemployed are concentrated. Does capital seek investment when there is the constant threat that the risks of investment are not the risks incident to the ordinary conduct of business, but incident to a deliberate governmental policy? Will capital seek investment, has it sought investment under a policy which must inevitably, just as surely as the night follows the day, if continued, destroy the currency? How then, if under a deliberate spending program threatening the destruction of the currency, is it reasonable to anticipate that capital will not seek investment. And if, therefore, the 60 per cent of the unemployed concentrated in the industries which depend upon capital investment cannot be restored to employment—how then, can spending encourage a real recovery?

So when one takes all of these factors into consideration, it seems to me that the whole argument that the budget will be balanced, given a recovery, falls to the ground; first, because the revenue will not be sufficient to meet expenditures, and second, because a deliberate excessive spending policy probably will not induce recovery except perhaps a hollow one—one which rests upon the sands and is as empty as a blown-out eggshell.

Thus, if the spending policy of the Administration is pursued with even a modicum of its present vigor, I see no reason to expect that we in the United States will be immune from the disastrous effects of previous experiences with such a policy, and that arising out of the consequences of the cheap money and spending policies just as out of the consequences of the efforts to regiment, there will emerge the great issue, whether we have the will to preserve our American institutions, or whether we lack the strength to preserve them. I recognize that the ultimate effects of a spending and cheap money policy may be long retarded, that there are many elements in the present situation which may delay their expression. For example, there no longer exist any of the known tests of government credit. There is no

secure place in the world for capital to go to. There
are at the disposal of the government many instrumentalities with which it may for some period of
time be able to support government credit at its artificial level. But equally as important is the fact that
everywhere men want to believe—probably never so
much as now—that nothing bad can happen in the
United States.

Moreover, it is probably true that there is prevalent the thought that our great stock of gold is a
guaranty against the serious consequences of continuous spending. For these reasons, the ultimate
consequences may be long retarded, though the situation is so complicated, the ramifications of regimentation are so great, the foreign currency situation
with its reflections upon our own economy so complicated, that some occurrence, either material to or
quite outside the field of finance may bring the whole
matter to a climax. It is conceivable, too, that the
very strong natural forces for recuperation may become so overwhelming that, notwithstanding acts of
government, we may experience something which
has the superficial appearances of recovery.

But because a cessation of government spending
during such a period would induce deflation and bring
such artificial "recovery" to an end—something
which few politicians have the courage to face—and
because of the vested interests created by spending
and because a mere recovery cannot increase revenues sufficiently to meet expenditures, it is more
than probable, in fact it is reasonable to expect, that
government deficits will continue, notwithstanding

that we may experience something which is heralded as recovery. And when such "recovery" terminates and the bubble bursts, there will consequently be superimposed upon the ordinary effects of deflation, such as we experienced in 1930 to 1933, an obvious and apparent impairment of the credit of the government. Thus, even if there is this apparent "recovery," its only effect will be to delay the day of reckoning.

But there is another very remote possibility. By some miracle the budget may be brought into balance, a real recovery commenced, and an atmosphere of confidence engendered. To prevent another great credit inflation the base for which has been so superabundantly created by monetary tricks, devaluation, and the financing mechanism for government deficits, superhuman courage and integrity—greater courage than can be expected of politicians, will be required. If it is not exercised, and it is not reasonable to expect that it will be exercised, then another great deflation will probably be experienced, with all of its pain and suffering and human misery, and with a public debt which will not permit of the use of government credit.

Consequently, from whatever angle we approach the problem, if the spending policies are continued, regardless of what the interventions may be—whether an apparent recovery or a slow process of disintegration—the terrific impetus of the economic forces created by another inflation, either credit or fear, and another great deflation, by an insolvent Federal Reserve System, a bankrupt banking system, a de-

stroyed middle class, and no credit with which the
unemployed may be relieved, it is difficult to conceive
of the method by which we may escape at least temporarily from the despotism of a dictatorship. It is
for this reason that the present fiscal policy, if continued, accentuates the issue manifested in the various acts designed to create a planned economy.

IV

A Free People and a Free Economy

Before proceeding with the fourth and last lecture, let me recall briefly the substance of the previous ones. It has been pointed out that the Post-War system failed because it was a system of embargo tariffs which not only contributed to the destruction of world currencies, but which also tended to impoverish a large part of our population; because of an excessive incurment of debt—private as well as governmental—induced by an inflation; because of the artificial mechanisms, some illegal, some expressly granted by the Congress, for the elevation and maintenance of prices; because of the many rigidities which had crept into the economic system; and because of the confusion of moral values, which all cheap money or inflationary periods engender.

The fallacies of a planned economy, too, have been analyzed—its complete incompatibility with both freedom and equality and with the survival, existence and growth of a vital middle class; the universal poverty which it causes; the social evils which it intensifies; the despotism which it makes inevitable. And it has been shown, also, that the present pseudo-planned economy leads relentlessly into the complete autocracy and tyranny of the Collective State.

The fiscal policy, too, has been shown to be but another force which gives momentum to the movement toward the oppressive authoritarian social organism.

Thus the issue is clearly defined. Every act is approaching, from different angles, the same focal point.

Will we choose to subject ourselves—this great country—to the despotism of bureaucracy, controlling our every act, destroying what equality we have attained, reducing us eventually to the condition of impoverished slaves of the State? Or will we cling to the liberties for which man has struggled for more than a thousand years? It is important that we understand the magnitude of the issue before us.

While the general defects of the Post-War system have been enumerated, perhaps it will be of some help in meeting the issue to measure the accomplishments of the order under which we have been living for more than a century and a half. For it is not enough merely to list the defects without at the same time appraising the benefits.

During the span of fifteen decades, under a system somewhat impaired by man's folly, made somewhat rigid by misunderstandings, we have nevertheless seen a small nation develop into one of the great powers of the world. We have witnessed thirteen colonies—a fringe along the Atlantic Seaboard—push on and expand into forty-eight great commonwealths. We have developed a great continent and we have attained the highest standard of living the world has ever known.

Two striking illustrations of this within the memory of living men are to be found in the increase in the number and distribution of automobiles and radios. In 1913 there were about 1¼ million registered motor vehicles, while in 1930 there were 26½ million. In 1923 there were approximately two million families who owned radios, while in 1930 there were some 12 million, and in 1935 it was estimated that there were approximately 19 million radio families.[1]

While it is true that these two illustrations are not the ultimate of our attainments, and while, at the same time, it may very well be that there are still groups who have not attained in life the things which we would like to see them have, nevertheless the unquestionable and undeniable fact remains that the number in the United States in this category has been steadily and consistently decreasing throughout our history, and that we have attained a standard of living which, however much it can be improved, has exceeded the fondest hopes of man.

Coincident with this amazing and extraordinary material development, the scope and extent of human liberties, of individual rights, have not decreased. Before we discard the fundamentals under which we have attained this degree of human happi-

[1] Statistical Abstract of the United States, 1933 (U. S. Dept. of Commerce, Bureau of Foreign and Domestic Commerce), p. 336. "Motor Vehicle Registrations, Passenger Cars and Motor Trucks Combined."

Estimated number of radio families obtained from National Broadcasting Company, New York (1935 estimate furnished NBC by McGraw-Hill Publishing Co., N. Y.).

ness and this extent of freedom for a system which ends only in tyranny, we should, it seems to me, carefully examine the extent to which modification of the old system can be made without impairing the rights of man to reach out toward a greater future.

In the light, then, of the destructive policies of the present and of both the sins and the virtues of the past, it is not inappropriate or irrelevant to attempt to enumerate the elements necessary to a liberal economy, a free people, and to a more successful operation of the American tradition.

If we do not elect to have a tyrannical, oppressive bureaucracy controlling our lives, destroying progress, depressing the standard of living, and, if under a democracy it is impossible to regiment, to regulate completely all industrial and agricultural activities of a nation without destroying, in part if not in whole, the individuals and groups of individuals engaged in those activities, then should it not be the function of the Federal government under a democracy to limit its activities to those with which a democracy may adequately deal, such for example as national defense, maintaining law and order, protecting life and property, preventing dishonesty, and finally compelling competition and guarding the public against the economic abuse and social waste of monopolies and vested special interests?

If, under a democracy or any other sort of a political system, it is impossible for governments directly or indirectly to operate a noncompetitive system for the full benefit and satisfaction of mankind, then should not democracies attempt to compel a competitive system with its automatic controls which, by their own momentum and forces turn on the danger signal and automatically register safety?

We must elect, as our ultimate goal, State ownership of all means of production—a static society and tyranny on the one hand, or we must elect private ownership of property—a progressively rising standard of living, a competitive society, and freedom on the other.

If we elect the latter, the problem is to make it work better, more smoothly, with fewer "booms" and fewer "busts," with a greater distribution of goods and with a greater opportunity for attaining positions of relative eminence—in short, to attain its more effective operation for the welfare of mankind.

The postulates to a smoother working of a liberal economy are, it seems to me: first, free competition and flexibility of prices; second, mobility of labor and of goods; third, flexibility of costs; fourth, a modification of our tariff policy to effect and maintain (a) a balance between agriculture and industry, (b) a sound currency, and (c) escape from despotism; fifth, a greater use of the "Compact Clause" of the Constitution and a greater exercise of local responsibility; sixth, a reformed banking system; and, finally, a responsible fiscal policy which will assure stability of exchanges.[1]

---

[1] Some may argue that this is as much government intervention as is a planned economy, or that what is here proposed, insofar as government intervention is concerned, differs from a planned economy only in degree. It seems to me however that there is a great dif-

On these *major* things and on these *major* things alone can individual security, higher standards of living, a really abundant life, freedom and liberty be attained. The first postulate to a successful liberal economy is competition and flexibility of prices.

One of the irrefutable, unanswerable arguments for capitalism is that it has inherent in it the competitive forces which compel the production of more goods at lower prices and which therefore compel the distribution of wealth. For it is only by producing more commodities for less that wealth can be distributed without destroying wealth. This, after all, is what capitalism has done for the United States. It was the competitive forces in the automobile industry which compelled the production of more automobiles at lower prices, thus making automobiles available to a larger number of people. It was the competitive forces in the refrigeration industry which compelled the production of automatic refrigerators at lower prices, thus making refrigerators available to a larger number of people. And so it has been throughout our economy. The highly competitive industries have produced more goods at lower prices and therefore have effected a greater distribution of wealth and a higher standard of living. It has been the restless energies of indi-

ference between government intervention to compel freedom and competition on the one hand and government intervention to prevent freedom and competition on the other, between a government's acting as an umpire of a game played by others under a certain simple set of rules, and the government participating itself as a player in the game.

vidual man's creative genius, set free and compelled to operate by the momentum of automatic competitive forces, which has raised us up out of the slough of the Middle Ages and the poverty of the Mercantile System.

It has, however, been previously pointed out, that during the Post-War period certain abuses crept in to the competitive system. The industrialist and the capitalist, through illegally fixing prices, gradually destroyed the competitive forces which justified the system in which they professed to believe. In some measure, at least, this, too, is what they were doing when they demanded and received of the Congress embargo tariffs—tariffs designed not to protect the efficient producer, but to protect the inefficient and the marginal producers. This, too, is what they have done in insisting upon price fixing provisions and provisions for the restriction of production in the N. R. A. Codes.

In doing these things they are false to the system in which they think they believe, to the system which socially has distributed wealth to a greater extent than wealth ever before in history has been distributed. They are unwittingly torpedoing a great social order and unconsciously undermining themselves. They have not the courage and the vitality to face the rigors of the system which they profess to worship.

Another method of stating the case is to discuss the second part of the first postulate to a successful operation of the profit system, i.e., flexibility of prices.

Given monopolistic practices of restricting production and a rigid price generally designed to protect the marginal producer, capital attains a profit—a return—at least temporarily guaranteed. A security is obtained, not resting on more effective and cheaper production, but on a position sheltered from the forces of competition. There is, therefore, no restless urge, no necessity for the creative instinct of man and of capital to seek employment in manufacturing more goods at a lower price. Capitalism, if it is to operate successfully, must be relatively flexible. This flexibility has been discouraged by monopolies and especially protected groups. Thus the construction trades and the heavy industries lag and thus employment is denied. Contrast this with a relatively free competitive system under which capital is constantly moving and populations are constantly shifting; under which, when it is thought that a certain commodity can be produced cheaper in a different locality than the one in which the commodity is then being produced, capital seeks investment in that different locality, labor is employed, construction materials are used, heavy industries prosper. If the new enterprise is successful people are employed permanently. New industrial areas are created. New houses are built to provide homes for the population of a new area. If it be successful, then it produces more goods at lower prices for consumption either by capital or by individuals. The interesting thing is not the security of a given block of capital, but the hazard which capital everywhere takes as a function in society not only of taking the risk of a profit, but also either temporarily or permanently of employing labor. It is not important what happens to one block of capital, to one particular portion of capital. It is mightily important, however, that capital perform its function. Monopolistic practices prevent it.

On the other hand, by whatever method attained—monetary or otherwise—price fixing, without other monopolistic practices, creates, as we should have learned from previous experience, the illusion of excessive security, and capital investment, at least partially obtained directly or indirectly through the channels of bank credit, is made in excessive amounts; excessive debt therefor is incurred; a "boom"—an inflation—is induced; eventually the appearance of overproduction is created; profits decline; unemployment begins to appear; and a deflation ensues.

Contrast this with the relatively free competitive system in which there does not exist an atmosphere of false security for capital, in which prices are controlled by competition. Under such a set of conditions capital is invested when, in a given area, it is thought that a commodity can be produced and distributed for less, or when there is the reasonable chance of profit in the production of a new product either to satisfy a new human want or in the more efficient manufacture of an article already being produced.

Thus price fixing, when wedded to other monopolistic practices, prevents the free movement of capital and labor, retards employment, hinders progress, weighs heavily on the consumer, and eventually leads to general unemployment. While, on the other hand, price fixing without other monopolistic practices induces a "boom," with its excessive debt, weighs heavily on the consumer, and is followed by painful deflation and unemployment.

Moreover, as has been previously discussed, rigid prices, either with or without monopolistic protection, attained both by tariffs and by price fixing, encourage the tendency toward the concentration of the means of production into fewer hands.

Finally, industrial price fixing tends to create a discrepancy between agricultural and industrial income and, therefore, an industrial and agricultural depression. To fix prices for agricultural commodities not only has the effect previously referred to in the case of cotton, but also makes more violent the disease sought to be cured. Consequently, to move toward a balance between agriculture and industry requires a cessation of price fixing.

The second postulate to a successful liberal economy is mobility of labor and of goods.

There must also be a free movement of labor, for just as price fixing may give to capital a sense of security and, therefore, destroy the urge and the incentive for mobility and investment, consequently denying employment, so an artificially high fixation of compensation for the unemployed diminishes the incentive to find employment, thereby reducing the productivity of the whole economy.

Neither capital nor labor seek employment when there is no motive to compel the search. Thus, all devices which destroy individual incentive should be avoided, for on them rest individual economic independence, the production of more goods, lower prices, and a distribution of wealth.

Whenever the free movement of goods is checked by destroying competition in the field of transportation, by artificially elevating the cost of production in one area to the level of that in another, or by arbitrarily imposing barriers (as has been done in the coal industry), then the opportunity for the employment of capital and of labor, and for individual economic independence, diminishes.

The third postulate to a successful liberal economy is flexibility of costs. This raises the dilemma of either flexible costs or a flexible currency. In view of our Post-War experience with a managed currency and in view of the recent attempts to cure the evils of a managed currency by more management— in view of the established fact that no political group, unless they be endowed with magnificent courage and great integrity, can hold their political supremacy and apply the necessary brakes at the proper time—in view of these demonstrated evils of a managed currency, we can not, without the expectancy of another "boom" and another terrific "bust," advocate flexibility of the monetary unit. And so we are driven to the other horn of the dilemma—flexibility of costs.

A general price level falls—either because of the more efficient competitive production of goods, or because an inflationary period has come to an end and a period of deflation begins, not infrequently intensified, as in the present depression, by national and international monetary chaos. If prices fall because of the first reason, the decline is gradual—there is no disequilibrium between prices and costs—and more wealth is distributed. If they fall for the latter, then disequilibrium between profits and costs exists and diminished profits and unemployment begin to appear.

Under a capitalistic, or any sort of a system, it can not reasonably be expected that we will not experience, in some measure at least, valleys and peaks, periods of higher prices caused by inflation, and periods of lower prices caused by deflation. One of the most effective ways to prevent the valleys from becoming too deep is hastily to adjust costs to prices.

When the price level begins to decline more than is justified by increased efficiency of production, profits begin to disappear. Production diminishes and unemployment increases. If adjustments in cost can immediately be made, profits become more probable, production increases, and unemployment decreases. This, it seems to me, is a fundamental and basic truth ignored in this depression by governments, by capitalists, and by labor leaders.

Three major elements of cost which tend to remain rigid are: (1) interest on capital, (2) wages for labor and (3) tax charges. It has been the practice in the United States, during the last 15 years, to resort more and more to the fixed obligation with a specified rate of interest—the bond—as a method of obtaining capital. Thus, in ever-increasing measure, the cost of capital in the United States has tended to become rigid. In Great Britain, on the other hand, the equity or stock on which there is no fixed charge has been the more common method of obtaining capital.[1] While for certain purposes the bond is a legitimate instrument for obtaining capital and by many investors is sought in preference to a stock, nevertheless, a greater use of the equity, of the common stock, as a method of obtaining capital, would diminish, in

[1] NEW CAPITAL ISSUES, UNITED STATES AND UNITED KINGDOM

Including Refunding but Excluding All Government Issues

	Total (Millions)	Bonds		Stocks	
		Amount (Millions)	% of Total	Amount (Millions)	% of Total
United States:					
1927...........	$8,551	$5,902	69	$2,648	31
1928...........	9,391	4,453	47	4,938	53
1929...........	11,248	3,213	29	8,035	71
1930...........	5,835	3,955	68	1,880	32
1931...........	2,573	2,243	87	330	13
1932...........	848	788	93	60	7
1933...........	329	113	34	216	66
1934...........	1,285	1,021	79	264	21
United Kingdom:					
1927...........	£222	£96	43	£126	57
1928...........	229	73	32	156	68
1929...........	190	42	22	148	78
1930...........	133	95	72	38	28
1931...........	59	32	54	27	46
1932...........	63	44	68	19	32
1933...........	65	42	65	23	35
1934...........	116	50	43	66	57

(Standard Statistics Co. Compilations; London Economist Compilations)

large measure, rigid capital costs and would, therefore insofar as it is concerned, inject a greater flexibility into our economy. As has been previously pointed out, during the first years of the depression it was urged by governments that wages be not reduced. Thus, in this respect, costs became rigid and what might otherwise have been a depression of ordinary severity was converted into one of the most intense, if not the most intense, in the history of modern nations. If labor leaders would but transfer the emphasis from increased wages to increased employment, if they would be responsible enough to those whose interests they are charged with protecting, if they would insist upon a flexibility of a wage scale, higher wages during periods of prosperity and a reduction at the inception of a depression, then the peaks might be leveled and the valleys might be raised.

Moreover, during the Post-War and depression periods, States, counties and municipalities contracted an excessive amount of indebtedness with the consequence of higher and rigid taxes to service the debt contracted. Thus, a further rigidity of cost was injected into the system, making adjustment of costs to prices more difficult, requiring in industry a further reduction of wages, or in agriculture bearing down with violence upon the farmer who had the greatest adjustment to make. Will not the political subdivisions in the future look with suspicion on proposals to increase debt, thus permitting of greater flexibility of costs, at least in so far as taxes are concerned? Will not the capitalist, the industrialist and labor dissolve the conspiracy into which they have unwittingly and jointly entered for the destruction of a liberal economy? Will not the capitalist be willing to face the tests of the system in which he says he believes, will he not be willing to accept more flexible return on investment, and will not labor be willing to acquiesce in the flexibility of costs so necessary to that liberal economy? If they are not, if both remain blind to the nature of freedom and of liberty, to the nature of the system which has done more for mankind than any other one, then we can not look forward with any confidence to the future. On the contrary, we may be compelled to accept the tyranny and the brutality of a Collective State—a dictatorship.

The fourth postulate to the successful operation of a liberal economy is a modification of our tariff policy, for upon it rests, among other things, a balance between agriculture and industry, a sound currency and escape from dictatorship.

In the United States, before the depression, about twenty per cent of our wheat crop was exported. Almost fifty per cent of our pork products was sold in the world market. About forty per cent of our tobacco crop was exported. And, up to the time of the Agricultural Adjustment Administration and the price fixing endeavors of the last two years (merely a continuation in a different form of the price fixing endeavors of 1930 and 1931), more than fifty-five per cent of our cotton crop was exported. It may be that because of our own folly during the Post-War period we will never again be an exporter of wheat and of pork products. It may be that because of the follies of the last two years we can never regain our foreign markets for cotton. It is not the course of wisdom, however, with respect to either, to adopt a defeatist's attitude, for the spectacle of defeat—an impoverished Southland and Middle West, with all of its ramified effects on our industrial areas—is too appalling to permit it. How then, can there be made the attempt to regain those foreign markets? What is the nature of foreign trade? Over a long period of years it must rest upon a mutual exchange of goods or their equivalent. If this be correct, and I believe it to be, then it is impossible to maintain any degree of foreign trade if one country refuses to be paid in goods and yet expects other countries to buy its goods. There can be no purchaser if the seller refuses to be paid. Yet this is precisely what we have done, for our embargo tariff policy prevents other countries from buying our domestic surpluses. There must, therefore, be a modification in our tariff policy. We cannot expect to have a prosperous agricultural area, either a prosperous cotton South or Middle West, if our tariff policy is such as to prevent the importation of goods in sufficient quantities to pay for our exports. This does not mean a policy of free trade. It does not mean that all tariffs must be immediately removed. Even if it did mean this, the damage which would be done to our national economy would probably no more than offset the good which would follow. For this country, in part at least, has developed its industrial economy behind protective tariffs. It does mean, however, a wise, maturely considered and carefully executed change in direction toward general reduction of our present high rates, made doubly high by the act of devaluing the dollar. That this is a difficult task to undertake cannot be denied, that the interests already vested will strenuously resist is a foregone conclusion unless they have miraculously developed a cosmic point of view rather than an atomic one, but that the prosperity of our great agricultural exporting population, of the Middle West and South—and, for that matter, of our entire country—depends on it, is almost beyond question.

A reduction of rates does not necessarily mean a lower wage scale. For example, in the United States there are produced the cheapest automobiles in the world, of which we export a substantial part of our production, and yet in the automobile industry the wages are higher than wages paid in the same industry in other parts of the world. Nor does a reduction in tariffs mean a lower standard of living, for even if it mean a lower general wage scale it would also mean lower prices and a greater exchange of goods, on which the standard of living rests. Nor does it mean more unemployment, though it would mean a shifting of labor and capital from inefficient plants and industries to the more efficient ones.[1]

[1] It seems to me that just as in the Mercantile Era of the 17th and 18th Century we now confuse wealth with money. Wealth is really goods. The greater the exchange of goods the greater is the wealth. The United States—the greatest free trade area in the world in which the greatest exchange of goods occurs and in which the highest standard of living has been attained—tends to confirm this conclusion.

There are, of course, certain special situations arising out of a deliberately and planned depreciated currency of a competitor nation. These special cases can be adequately dealt with, it seems to me, by other methods, such, for example, as anti-dumping provisions to prevent importation from countries which have deliberately depreciated their currency and which refuse to enter into an accord to bring monetary order out of the present chaos.

I do not say that a modification of our tariff policy alone would necessarily regain for the South a foreign market for its cotton, which it is now bidding fair to lose. The Agricultural Adjustment Administration and the price fixing program have encouraged the clearance of land in Brazil, the conversion of coffee plantations into cotton plantations. The South, therefore, is now confronted with a competition with which it was not previously faced. If, therefore, the opportunity, through a modification of tariff policy, is given to the South to regain its export market, then it will be squarely up to the South to decide whether it will accept it. Should it decide to make the effort, it must undertake to reduce its costs to meet the competition which the government has created. And this means, among other things, a reduction in State taxes, for taxes are an important element of cost in agricultural production. At any rate, the government, having created a competitor for the South, should now acknowledge its mistake by extending to the South the opportunity once again to compete for its market.

But there is another reason equally as powerful if not more powerful for a modification of our tariff policy. No creditor nation can long continue to export more than it imports without eventually draining from the rest of the world a large portion of its gold stocks, thus contributing to chaos in the exchange markets and inducing a deflation in our domestic economy. When England was forced to abandon gold, and sterling during the six month period from June 1 to December 1, 1931, fell against the dollar from $4.87 to $3.37, the price of cotton and of wheat fell from nine cents per pound and 68 cents per bushel respectively, to 6.3 cents per pound and 52 cents per bushel.[1] The stock market declined correspondingly, other values decreased rapidly, unemployment here increased and the vicious movement of deflation reached its climax. These, too, were substantially the same effects on economies of other countries, caused by the arbitrary devaluation of the dollar—deflationary forces were intensified elsewhere, futile devices were employed to protect economies—the volume of trade decreased and unemployment increased.

Aside from any theoretical consideration, experience alone, therefore, demonstrates that there must be stability of exchanges for the successful operation of the capitalistic system or, for that matter, of any system. No country can pursue the policies which the United States pursued from 1922 through 1930

[1] Sterling, demand value; cotton, middling spot N. Y.; Wheat, No. 2 Hard Winter Spot, Kansas City.

without creating chaos in the exchange markets and subjecting its own internal economy to terrific shocks and its own people to great suffering.

We have learned that by making foreign loans over a limited period of time we can continue to be a creditor, continue to have a favorable balance of trade without immediately destroying currencies, but this process can be continued only for a limited period, for eventually the constantly cumulating foreign loans create cumulative return payments and therefore cumulative demand for dollars which, under excessively high tariffs, can not be satisfied through goods sold in the United States and which must, therefore, eventually be settled with gold.

The continuous flow of gold in one direction drains gold from the countries which import our exports and from which gold is exported to us for the purpose of making purchases. This process may go on for a certain period, but eventually the country whose stocks of gold are being continuously diminished is confronted either with a complete abandonment of the gold standard or devaluation. The first step in chaos of exchanges then takes place and the first step in the direction of continuous deflation in this country is taken, for the country which has depreciated its exchange generally imposes tariffs in a futile effort to stimulate exports, restrict imports, create for itself a favorable balance of payments, and thus to reverse the flow of gold. It, then, may have a purely temporary advantage if it is one of our competitors in foreign markets for, by means of depreciation, its export prices are lower and, because more units of its currency are required to purchase dollars with which to purchase our goods, our exports diminish. There is consequently created a dislocation in our own internal economy; the price of our exportable commodities falls to compensate for the depreciation of the foreign currency and our internal economy is thrown out of equilibrium. Profits then begin to disappear. If costs of production are diminished, then the drain of gold from the foreign purchasing country to us continues and foreign currencies depreciate further until the deflation of prices becomes so great at home that we are compelled, by the pressure of economic forces, to depreciate our currency. This in turn creates deflationary forces elsewhere; it encourages the depreciation of additional foreign currencies in retaliation and the whole world becomes engaged in an intense economic warfare in which the implements of destruction are depreciated exchanges, tariffs, exchange restrictions and quotas. Nationalistic sentiments are aroused, internal and world economies are thrown completely out of equilibrium. Trade diminishes, unemployment increases, and human suffering is intensified.

Moreover, this would be equally true were the world to adopt a managed money. For the external value of a currency would depend entirely on supply and demand. Were exports to exceed imports or were the balance of payments to be favorable, then the demand for dollars would be greater than the supply and the dollar would either appreciate or foreign currencies would depreciate.

The industrialists, therefore, who are constantly

seeking higher and higher tariffs with one breath and who are shouting for a sound currency with another, are demanding two irreconcilable things, granting that the United States either continues to be a creditor nation or becomes a financial neutral.

But there may be some who advocate a closed economy, a completely isolated one. Not only does this mean a diminution of the supply of things which we need and therefore a lowered standard of living, not only does it mean the impoverishment of the South, the corn belt, and the great manufacturing areas which produce for export; it means more than this, for, as has been so ably pointed out by Professor Gustav Cassel in the Richard Cobden Lecture for 1934, entitled "From Protectionism through Planned Economy to Dictatorship," and as has been so clearly revealed by our own recent experiences, a closed economy leads eventually to a despotic State. Either we must alter our tariff policy to bring our economy into balance, to maintain a sound currency and to enjoy some measure of the rights of man, or we must submit to the inevitable tyranny which follows unmistakably from an isolated economy.

To state the case differently, it seems clear, then, that an equilibrium between agriculture and industry, stability of exchanges, an escape from despotism, are essential requirements of a liberal system. It is for this reason that a modification of our tariff policy, undertaken temperately and with great wisdom so as to produce the least and the shortest shock to our economy and so as to provide the element of time necessary to readjustment, is a pre-requisite to a successful free economy in the United States. This conclusion is not predicated solely upon theoretical considerations. It is confirmed by an analysis of our Post-War and depression experience. We can not have our pie and eat it too. We can not live a life of isolation without impoverishing, at least, agriculture. We can not build around our economy unscalable tariff walls and long maintain a sound dollar. We can not live within ourselves and long retain our human liberties. It is not here intended to give to our export trade a greater emphasis than it deserves nor is it intended that our export trade should be considered to be more important than our domestic market. It would be a misrepresentation of fact to attempt to give this impression, but it is intended to point out that there can be no prosperity in the ten principal cotton producing States,[1] in the corn and hog belt, and in many other agricultural

[1] According to the Statistical Abstract of the United States for 1933 (U. S. Dept. of Commerce, Bureau of Foreign & Domestic Commerce) cotton acreage in the 10 principal cotton producing States was as follows:

	1 9 3 2	
	Acres Thousands	Farm Value 1,000 dollars
Entire U. S.	35,939	405,751
Texas	13,334	139,500
Mississippi	3,839	38,500
Arkansas	3,378	40,474
Oklahoma	3,108	30,894
Alabama	3,021	29,831
Georgia	2,651	27,328
Louisiana	1,688	19,552
S. Carolina	1,661	23,270
N. Carolina	1,251	21,780
Tennessee	1,064	14,640

areas, unless the American people are willing, in the public interest, to support a program for wise and temperate modification of tariff policy. It is intended to point out that we cannot long maintain a sound currency, if we ever again have one, unless the American people are willing, in the public interest, to support a program for wise and temperate modification of tariff policy. And it is intended to point out that we cannot avoid a dictatorship unless the American people are willing, in the public interest, to support a program for wise and temperate modification of tariff policy.

The fifth postulate to a successful liberal economy is preservation of local responsibility and a greater use of the "Compact Clause" of the Constitution, which makes permissible, subject to the consent of Congress, treaties among States, having to do with problems which are inter-state in character, but which are not national in scope. It is susceptible of great use in the solution of such questions without creating in Washington a bureaucracy reaching its mighty arms into every corner of our land. It keeps responsibility and administration close to the people of the geographical areas at interest.

In the matter of labor and social legislation, it may well be the most effective instrument to employ.

With respect to labor legislation, I think it is important not to forget that in a liberal economy there is the danger that capital may, to too great an extent, absorb profits at the expense of labor. In most respects there is a community of interest between these two productive forces in society, but to protect one against the other may be a function of government. Labor should be protected, without coercion from *any source,* in its right to organize in such a way as individual men may think advisable, to bargain collectively without dictation from government and, through this right, to guard *intelligently*—and I use this word advisedly—its interests. But this may not be enough. A minimum wage may be a necessary statutory limitation. Remembering, however, the dangers inherent in a Federal bureaucracy ruling from afar the actions of a people, the States acting as independent units or in geographical groups, through the "Compact Clause" of the Constitution, should establish the measure of the minimum, always keeping in mind that the minimum should be so established as to retain the greatest possible flexibility of costs, and full mobility of capital, labor and goods. Nationwide standards are not only unworkable but have great social and economic consequences. The standard of living in various geographical areas varies widely, climatic conditions are quite dissimilar and living costs are not constant. For this reason, a nationwide limitation is not a desirable thing. Moreover, a nationwide minimum tends to elevate costs in one area to the level of more costly areas, thus tending to stop a flow of capital and to retard employment. And, besides, it may have profound consequences on agricultural regions.

But wherever a State elects to establish a standard it should be free to do so. And wherever groups of States with common conditions elect to establish a minimum they should be free to utilize the provisions of the Constitution which permit them to make treaties among themselves subject always to the consent of Congress.[1]

Since there has been much public agitation on the general subject of social security legislation, it is not amiss to briefly discuss it here.

It can be safely assumed that almost all are emotionally stirred in favor of legislation which will give a measure of security against unemployment and old age. It is, however, important to realize that often when an act is taken under the pressure of emotional zeal, it is subsequently, in the light of reason, proven to be harmful. So it may well be with hasty legislation designed to attain social security. Since flexibility of costs, mobility of labor and of capital are essential to individual freedom and a Liberal Economy, any social security legislation must be so designed as to retain the incentive on the part of Labor and Capital to seek employment, and so as to prevent the injection of another cost rigidity and another fixture into our economy.

Reformation of the banking system is the sixth postulate to a more successful operation of the competitive system of a free people. Two basic and fundamental reforms, it seems to me, are necessary. An analysis of the Post-War period discloses the facts that when the Chicago Federal Reserve Bank refused to lower its rediscount rate in 1927, the Fed-

---

[1] In a speech delivered at the Jefferson Day Banquet in New York City, April 20, 1929, reprinted in the Congressional Record, Vol. 71, Part 2, p. 1169, 71st Congress, 1st Session, this point of view was presented at greater length by the author.

eral Reserve Board, acting under political influence, vetoed its action. Moreover, when in early 1929 the various Federal Reserve Banks recognized the serious consequences of the cheap money policy and sought to correct the evils by raising the rediscount rate, again the Federal Reserve Board, acting under political influence, offered strong and effective resistance.[1] Our experience with State owned banks confirms our recent experiences. Thus, history tends to prove the conclusion that politicians seldom, if ever, consciously undertake to stop a "boom." For their election depends upon its continuance.

They may recognize that the "boom" may be followed by a "bust" which may throw them out of office. But notwithstanding whatever understanding they may entertain of the consequences, it is but human for them to continue on the inflationary course in the romantic Micawberish hope that "something will turn up" to prevent the deflation.

In the present situation, with excess reserves of the Federal Reserve System piled up to a height which must make any thoughtful person gasp with apprehension, with an Administration which is openly and frankly committed to inflation as an instrument of recovery, with a low money rate artificially created by Treasury and general governmental policy, with the Federal Reserve System holding 2.5 billions of dollars of government obligations and the commercial banks holding about 11

[1] "Monetary Mischief," by George Buchan Robinson, published after these lectures were delivered, gives a clear account of this controversy.

billions, is it conceivable that the dominant political party will permit the Federal Reserve to raise the rediscount rate or to increase the reserve requirements, or to sell government obligations and thus destroy the inflationary recovery which it is attempting to induce? Such a policy would create a situation which must result in the defeat of the dominant party at the next election, and would therefore be an act of political madness. No politicians, however loud may be their protestations of righteousness, simply can not deliberately exercise a control except when the control is aimed at inflation. Yet these are some of the drastic steps which must be taken to prevent another New Era and Great Depression. Even these will be ineffective if the Budget remains out of balance.

That this is true is amply confirmed by our tragic experience with State owned banks during the terrific paper and credit inflation of the '30's of the last century. In fact, it is confirmed by almost every experience in history save one.

Consequently, political influence on and control of credit, having been proved, at least within our experience, to be conducive to "booms" and "busts," it is but the course of reason to remove the banks as far as possible from those whose positions are held by reason of political forces. This, it seems to me, is the first major reform to be made in our banking system.

A history of our great inflations—at least those not induced by government deficits—reveals, or seems to reveal, the fact that they have been caused in part by excessive use of bank credit, directly or indirectly, in capital loans, i.e., long time loans for capital purposes. The consequences have been, first, that capital borrowings have been made out of fiat credit rather than savings, second, excessive incurment of debt on capital account, individual, State, and corporate, and, third, that the expansion thus encouraged has accentuated both the "booms" and the "busts" and left the banks with a large volume of frozen assets which in turn have contributed to bank failures.

The theory of the pending banking bill [1] is consistent with our experience and makes possible an even greater use of bank credit for capital purposes than any we have had in recent years, for through its eligibility provisions, it is designed, as the Governor of the Board frankly states, to permit the member banks to discount with the system almost any conceivable type of loan. Thus, if the inflations of the past have been accentuated by the use of bank credit for capital purposes—and I believe they have been—then the pending bill will intensify the evils of the past.

The contrary method of attacking the problem is to revert to the original intent of the Federal Reserve Act of 1913 (so completely perverted during its existence of 22 years) and to establish as an objective the restriction of capital loans to savings and thus automatically to prevent the great "booms" and the great deflations. This probably can not be attained in full, for the complications are too great

[1] The Eccles Banking Bill of 1935.

and bank credit for capital purposes seeps out in too many different ways. But it can be approximated, as is evidenced by the experience of Great Britain, where, in more recent years, the use of bank credit for capital purposes is much less than in this country, and where bank failures have been negligible.

At any rate, these are the two opposite theories. Before doing one or the other, the whole subject should be most carefully studied and maturely considered—not behind closed doors—not in a star chamber proceeding, but rather in prolonged public hearings held for the purpose of honestly determining the best policy.

But equally important is that rules for playing the game be established and that those rules be rigidly and uncompromisingly followed—not changed, as in the past, when they began to be painful, for it is only by incurring slight and temporary pain that the violent fluctuations with their accompanying intense misery can be avoided! This—a lowering of the peaks and a raising of the valleys of our economic topography—a successful Liberal Economy requires.

The final postulate to a Liberal Economy is a fiscal policy designed to keep the expenditures of the Federal government within its income.

In the third lecture there were discussed the hazards of the present spending program, and the almost inevitable catastrophe to which it eventually leads.

Here it is proposed to explain the advantages of a balanced Budget, and how it can be attained.

The spending policy is predicated upon the theory that individual consuming power must be increased. It has been pointed out in a previous discussion that this conception rests upon the erroneous thought that the only consumption is that undertaken by individuals, and ignores the fact that capital, or savings, consumes under ordinary circumstances almost as much as do individuals. Moreover, it is this fallacy which is at the bottom of much prevalent economic thinking. An analysis of the depression shows clearly that the great vacuum in our economy is in the heavy goods industries which rests upon consumption by capital, or stated another way, capital investment for productive purposes. Capital does not seek investment unless there is confidence that it will not be destroyed by acts of governments, monetary, fiscal, or otherwise.

Thus the effect of a spending policy is possibly to increase individual consumption, with its ramifications upon a few consumers' goods industries. But because of the apprehension which it creates, it tends to diminish the amount of capital invested in the durable goods industries and so to retard employment for it is in the heavy industries, in which approximately 60 [1] per cent of our unemployed are now concentrated.

Thus the various acts of the Administration, budgetary, monetary and oppressive of business, are the reasons why business cannot proceed to perform

[1] Report to the President of the U. S. on National Recovery and Employment, by the Durable Goods Industries Committee, p. 10. (Based on estimate by Col. Ayres of Cleveland Trust Co.) Estimate made for March, 1934. Refined estimate 56%.

its normal function. Those who say that the government must spend because business has failed are in effect saying the government must spend, so that business can not perform its function.

If, then, the spending policy does not encourage recovery,—and it has been demonstrated that it does not,—and if it leads to a social and economic disaster, how may both recovery be encouraged and the disaster be avoided, at least within the field of fiscal policy?

Private capital seeks investment when an atmosphere of confidence is created—the evidence of this is the meaning of the word credit, from "credo," I believe, on which our economy rests.

Evidence of a grim determination to change the direction of fiscal policy—would destroy the fear of inflation, the fear that a continuous spending program would project the government further into the field of private enterprise—and would release for expenditure on productive purposes and therefore for the employment of the unemployed, more than 25 billions of dollars, the demand for which has been previously demonstrated. Those who seek the absorption of the idle in productive enterprise should weigh the great employing power of this expenditure against the employment in unproductive ventures which five billion dollars of government spending may cause.

In view of the fact that so many vested interests have been created by spending, that the present degree of recovery in the consumers' goods industries has been induced largely by spending, any such change in direction probably will induce deflation for a limited period of time, and subject the Administration which attempts it to a test of its courage and integrity. But the confidence which it would create —and no profit system can exist in an atmosphere of fear—would, within a short period of time, compensate for the reduction of government expenditures, for, as has been pointed out previously in these lectures, the demand for capital expenditure by private enterprise is enormous—at least five, and perhaps ten times as much as the expenditures by the government.

Nor would it be difficult, within a reasonable period of time, to bring the Budget into balance, for within a period of two years, given a cessation of expenditures on new public works which experience has demonstrated to be futile, a modified relief program, and given a conversion of the R. F. C. and other credit agencies into pure liquidating agencies, the Budget actually could be balanced and debt reduction commenced. That this is technically attainable is disclosed by the analysis of expenditures contained in the third lecture. Until this occurs, until the evidence of change in direction has been made apparent, we can expect no security and no permanent basic recovery.

Moreover, a successful operation of the competitive system requires stability of exchanges. There can be no revival of foreign trade without it, there can be no equilibrium of world economy without it and I doubt that the low hanging clouds of war will be dispelled without it—for its attainment would mean at least an armistice to an intense economic warfare. There can be no full prosperity in the United States without it, and, as a condition precedent to it there must be evidenced here a financial responsibility disclosed not by words, but by acts designed to bring our Budget into balance, for no responsible power can move in the direction of stabilization, thus risking its own currency and world recovery, with a power which has demonstrated a lack of responsibility.

A change of direction towards a really balanced Budget is, therefore, the essence of recovery, of our reemployment problem, of our monetary problem and is a vital element in a Liberal Economy.

This, then, in broad outline, is the sort of an economy—a Liberal Economy—in which the greatest distribution of wealth, the greatest human happiness, and the greatest amount of individual liberty and freedom can be had. It is not a planned economy in the sense that it is regulated and controlled with respect to wages, hours, prices, methods of labor, places of labor, quantity of savings, type of occupation, family life and place of worship, by a great cancerous bureau or group of bureaus, of a tyrannical government. Under it the free play of democratic, competitive forces and man's individual creative genius, resting upon a foundation of a certain limited number of governmentally established stable pre-requisites, will automatically and unconsciously operate a liberal system for a free people, just as unconsciously the breathing functions of man go on and make of him a living, vital being.

And now one final thing for which we must strive in the Liberal Economy—Security. This cannot be attained by legislation alone—this cannot be obtained by statutory provisions—this cannot be grasped from a relentless destiny by the enactment of laws. It is as futile to legislate security as it is to legislate that water must flow up hill. It can be attained only by insisting upon a liberal economy in which the free forces of competition—of man's creative genius—blaze the way and clear the path for employment and recovery. It can be attained only by resurrecting from the grave the old virtues—intense patriotism—a willingness to see the whole economy in which we operate—the character to stand upon our feet without the assistance of an ever-grasping government—the courage to acknowledge our mistakes and to pay the penalty for them. It can be attained not by ease, but by work. It can be attained not by spending, but by saving. It can be attained not by dictatorial State planning, but by competition. It can not be attained by wishing for it, but by developing the character, the integrity of purpose to grasp it. It can not be attained by imitating Russia, but by a renewed conviction in America.

It rests upon a free economy—no price fixing— flexibility of costs—a modified tariff policy—an independent, reformed banking system—a Balanced Budget—a sound currency.

These are not mere words, for they have hidden in them the human values and the human yearnings of a free people—the right to vote for whom one chooses—the assurance of a fair trial before one's peers—the opportunity to work where one chooses to work—the chance to open the roads to new industrial enterprise, to economic independence—the inalienable right to express one's views as and when one chooses—to marry whomever one elects to marry —to enjoy the happiness of a home and of its safety —to worship the God of one's selection. All these things—the rights of man—the dignity and the pride of a great race—are in them.

All these things—the cherished liberties of a thousand years of struggle—the most valuable treasures of mankind—are at stake. This is the Liberal Tradition.